HANDY
ANIMAL ID
GUIDES

Identifyir
Common British

Birds

This is a **FLAME TREE** book
First published in 2015

Publisher and Creative Director: Nick Wells
Senior Project Editor: Catherine Taylor
Picture Research: Victoria Lyle and Sonya Newland
Art Director: Mike Spender
Layout Design: Jane Ashley
Copy Editor: Sonya Newland
Proofreader: Dawn Laker
Indexer: Eileen Cox

Special thanks to: Laura Bulbeck

FLAME TREE PUBLISHING
Crabtree Hall, Crabtree Lane
Fulham, London SW6 6TY
United Kingdom

www.flametreepublishing.com

First published 2015

15 17 19 18 16
1 3 5 7 9 10 8 6 4 2

A CIP record for this book is available from the British Library upon request.

ISBN 978-1-78361-405-9

Printed in Singapore

Picture Credits:
Illustrations by **Ann Biggs**. FLPA: Terry Andrewartha: 37; Bill Baston: 39; Neil Bowman: 8, 50, 139, 151, 170, 199; Frans Van Boxtel: 90, 143; Jim Brandenburg: 157; Ben Van Den Brink: 86, 129, 198; Richard Brooks: 117, 126, 132, 148, 241; S Charlie Brown: 49, 58; Rino Burgio: 131; Michael Callan: 180; Robert Canis: 80 & 246 (r), 106, 113, 121; Justus de Cuveland: 124; Frits Van Daalen: 99, 123; Do Van Dijck: 56, 130, 185, 246 (l); R. Dirscherl: 164; Dickie Duckett: 25, 209; Danny Ellinger: 13 & 165, 172, 212, 223; Peter Entwistle: 83, 91; Yossi Eshbol: 43, 211; Otto Faulhaber: 87; Philip Friskorn: 61, 196; Tony Hamblin: 18, 41, 55, 63, 95, 120, 188; John Hawkins: 4 (b), 4 (t) & 46, 17, 45, 53, 67, 69, 72, 85, 100, 115, 147, 166, 195; Fred Hazelhoff: 75, 191; Paul Hobson: 12, 51, 66, 74, 96, 114, 144, 239; Adri Hoogendijk: 146; Michio Hoshino: 11; David Hosking: 22 & 169, 23, 39, 104, 122, 162, 193; Frits Houtkamp: 42; Michael Krabs: 229; Mike Lane: 20, 34, 70 & 89, 189, 208, 221, 225; Bob De Lange: 94; Frans Lanting: 10, 19, 248; S & D & K Maslowski: 181, 237; Phil McLean: 35, 76, 81, 105, 141, 178; Derek Middleton: 28, 77, 93, 125, 149; Oene Moedt: 220; Elliott Neep: 27; Mark Newman: 6, 159; Flip De Nooyer: 82, 135, 168, 215, 240; Fritz Polking: 231; L Lee Rue: 204; Cyril Ruoso: 243; Hans Schouten: 171; Malcolm Schuyl: 5 (t), 5 (b) & 156, 26, 145, 161, 179, 190, 207; Silvestris Fotoservice: 116, 186; Mark Sisson: 21, 64, 119; Wim Smeets: 245; Jan Smit: 214; Gary K Smith: 44, 160, 217; Jurgen & Christine Sohns: 15, 33, 175, 177; Krystyna Szulecka: 227, 233; Roger Tidman: 24, 40, 60, 111, 128, 176, 194; Tom Vezo: 219, 235; Maurice Walker: 97; John Watkins: 54, 102, 103, 163; Michael Weber: 174; Wim Weenink: 57, 142; Roger Wilmshurst: 14, 47, 48, 79, 98, 101, 127, 133, 137, 183, 222; Winfried Wisniewski: 167, 205, 210; Martin Woike: 59, 197, 203, 213; John Van Der Wouw: 134; Bernd Zoller: 16, 173. **Shutterstock.com**: Donna Apsey: Enlightened Media: 200; Erni: 52; 31; Evgeni Stefanov: 155; Mark Bridger: 109; Menno Schaefer: 65; Mircea BEZERGHEANU: 73; Panu Ruangjan: 187; S.Cooper Digital: 32; taviphoto: 152

HANDY
ANIMAL ID
GUIDES

Identifying
Common British

Birds

DAVID CHANDLER, DOMINIC COUZENS, RUSS MALIN & STEPHEN MOSS

**FLAME TREE
PUBLISHING**

Contents

How to Use This Book 6

Introduction 10

Identifying Birds 14

Features to Look For 14

What to Beware of 22

Urban and Suburban Species 28

Woodland Species 70

Open Country Species 106

Freshwater and

   Marshland Species 152

Coastal Species 200

Useful Addresses 246

Further Reading 247

Glossary 249

Index of Latin Names 253

General Index 254

How to Use This Book

This book is a simple introduction to identifying species of birds that you are likely to encounter without too much trouble or expertise, whether in your back garden or out on a walk in the woods.

Identifying Birds

This section offers a brief guide to the key things to look for when bird-watching: what features to look out for when trying to identify birds – and what to beware of – and where to go both locally and abroad.

The Species

The species are broken down into sections organized by habitat. There is an entry on all the key common birds of Britain and Europe, organized within each section according to family groups. Every entry is accompanied by a handy box with a series of facts:

Size

Gives the approximate size range of the adult species.

Population

This gives a rough idea of how common – or scarce – the species is, and thus how likely you are to come across it.

It is difficult to give specific figures for most species of bird, for obvious reasons, so instead standard

terminology is used to describe the species populations, from rare, through common winter visitor, for example, to abundant.

Small
(up to 15 cm/
5⅞in)

Medium
(16–30 cm/
6¼–11⅞ in)

Medium-large
(31–45 cm/
12¼–17¾ in)

Large
(46–70 cm/
18–27⅝i in)

Very large
(71 cm/
28 in and over)

Scientific Name
This gives the bird's Latin or scientific name – the name by which it is classified by experts.

Identifying Features
These are suggested features to look out for when trying to distinguish one bird from another. Many birds – even those of a different group – may look similar from a distance or when camouflaged by a tree canopy,

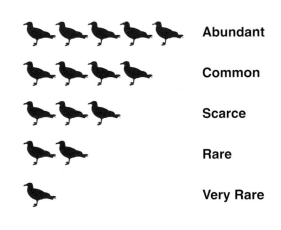

Abundant

Common

Scarce

Rare

Very Rare

for example. Remember that a bird's plumage may change between seasons and between sexes, and these changes are noted where considered relevant.

Similar Species

This is intended partly as a guide to other species in a group but also to suggest pitfalls when bird-watching – similar species can often be mistaken for one another.

This information is followed by an introductory summary of the bird, and then a lengthier description of its preferred habitats and plumage, and its habits such as courting, mating, breeding, eating, nesting and the number of eggs that are typical.

Reference Section

At the end of the encyclopedia is a list of Useful Addresses, along with websites, with birding and wildlife organizations; there is also a list of Further Reading to expand on subjects and species

covered here. A Glossary explains any terms that might be unfamiliar, and two Indexes (Scientific names and Common Names) will allow you to instantly locate a particular species.

Habitat

Summarizes the range of places where the birds can be found. Often this is in more than one particular type of habitat – birds may choose to breed somewhere different from their preferred environment the rest of the time, for example.

Diverse

Oceans
Seas
Coasts

Towns
Cities
Urban areas
Suburban areas

Ponds
Lakes
Rivers
Gravel pits
Open water

Parkland
Gardens

Cliffs

Coniferous woodland
Deciduous woodland
Mixed woodland
Ancient woodland

Islands
Beaches

Open country
Farmland/ agricultural land

Upland and tundra
Mountains

Moorland
Heathland
Grassland
Meadows

Summer
visitor

Scrub Hedgerows

Reedbeds
Marshes

Winter
visitor

Introduction

Bird-watching is one of the best ways of relaxing and enjoying nature, and it can be an extremely rewarding pastime if you know what to look for and where. The birds of Britain and Europe offer a feast of opportunity and quite an astounding diversity. From the ubiquitous pigeon to the rare Scottish Crossbill (the only species endemic to the British Isles), the familiar Mallard to the elusive Snowy Owl, there is something to be discovered wherever you are.

The Basics

This book includes a small section to help you bear in mind key things to look out for when bird watching, before getting straight to the nitty gritty: the species you may be able to tick off your list!

The Species

The species are organized by habitat. This should enable the reader to understand the types of birds they will find in a particular area. Of course, birds are not stationary creatures and few confine themselves permanently to a single habitat – some may be prolific in an area during the breeding season but rare outside it. It can also be difficult to categorize habitats neatly. Some water birds do indeed inhabit areas with freshwater, but many will also confine themselves to these areas within woodland regions, for example. The migratory habits of particular species should also be taken into account. There are thus birds listed here that would comfortably fit into two or more habitat categories, so don't rule out a bird you think you have identified over farmland just because it appears in the Woodland section.

Sub-division

Within each habitat section, the birds are ordered by family groupings. This is the order proscribed by the British Ornithologists Union and other organizations, which allows birds to be seen with related species. Remember that just because a particular bird doesn't have the word 'duck' in its common name, does not mean it isn't a duck!

'Vital Stats'

Each entry is accompanied by a summary of key information – size, main habitats, population, scientific name, identifying features and similar species. The size of a bird will instantly enable the watcher to eliminate hundreds of species and focus on a particular size grouping, from small to very large. Habitats explains in more detail where the bird is likely to be seen. Population is intended as a guide to how likely you are to see a particular species. Actual bird populations are extremely difficult to measure and fluctuate wildly from year to year and indeed between seasons and locations, so here you will find out whether the bird is abundant or just a winter visitor, a common sight in the named habitats or a passage migrant (a non-breeding visitor).

Identification

It is important to remember when looking for identifying features that plumage can change dramatically between seasons, between the sexes, and indeed between juvenile and adult birds. In the Identifying Features tag at the beginning of each species entry we have noted where plumage descriptions relate to specific seasons or sexes, but the main text of each entry will give more detailed information about plumage and other identifying features. To aid with identification, we have also named similar species with which the relevant bird might be confused. Colour photographs of all the birds give an immediate idea of what the species looks like, but also bear in mind that a bird may not look exactly like the picture! Often using features such as wing bars and other characteristics can be the best way to distinguish one species from another.

A Solid Foundation

This book is intended as a guide to the interested amateur and should be used as a starting point for your bird-watching adventure. It is impossible to give every detail about every bird you are likely to encounter across this vast region, but those outlined offer a good range of the common types and families you might see. If your interest is piqued, investigate further by using one of the many excellent field guides available, which can be more specific. Today there is also a multitude of other media available to help you locate and identify birds – from CDs of birdsong to vast quantities of information on the Internet. At the back of this book are listed some of the best websites to look at to find out more about birds and bird-watching.

Identifying Birds

To enjoy a bird you do not need to know its name, but for most bird watchers, putting a name to what they are looking at is very important. For some, identification is the end point. Arguably though, it is just the beginning – work out what the bird is and you can begin to find out more about it. Bird identification is about detective work. Collect as many clues as possible and come to a conclusion – an identification that is 'beyond reasonable doubt'.

Features to Look For

A bird watcher with even a modicum of experience may appear to have remarkable powers of identification to someone just starting out on their bird-watching journey. A confident identification of a glimpsed bird or of a brief blast of birdsong may feel like an unattainable level of expertise. The truth is, though, that a successful identification is simply the result of processing the available information to reach a conclusion. Sometimes, with experience, this can be done very quickly and when you know what you're looking for, some birds are very easy to identify. At other times it can be a lengthier process. Identification can be difficult, but with practice it gets easier. Below are some features to look out for.

Size

Estimating the size of a bird is a good starting point. Books express a bird's size in centimetres or inches – this is its length from the tip of its bill, over its head and along its back to the tip of its tail. Clearly it is of limited use when you are looking at a bird hopping about in a bush. The trick is to

compare the bird with another that you know reasonably well. Is it about the size of a sparrow, thrush or pigeon for example?

Take care when interpreting the sizes given in books. They are useful for comparisons, but remember that a bird with a long bill or tail will, according to the book, be 'bigger' than a bird with a short bill or tail but have the same sized body.

Shape

Again, try to compare your mystery bird to one that you know. Even novice bird watchers will be surprised at how many bird shapes they already know: duck, heron, bird of prey, pheasant, owl, pigeon, gull, kingfisher, sparrow and crow perhaps. Getting its shape right will help you get to the right pages in your field guide.

Markings

Some birds have very obvious markings and these may be all that you need to see to identify the bird. In the UK, a pigeon with a white crescent across its wing has to be a Wood Pigeon. But sometimes

subtler features need to be checked to confirm an identification. Marsh Tit and Willow Tit look very similar (and were not even recognized as different species until the late 1800s). One feature that helps to separate them is the Willow Tit's pale wing panel, though their voice can be even more helpful.

Make a note of any obvious markings, and if you have time, try to describe the whole bird, from bill tip to tail tip. If you have a field guide with you and have a rough idea of what you might be looking at, you might want to have a quick look in the book before embarking on a lengthy description. Hopefully, the book will tell you what you need to check to sort out the identification and you can make that your priority, before the bird flies off. Traditional bird-watching 'wisdom' is that you should not work this way because the book may influence you to such a degree that you begin to see features on the bird that are not really there. This is a possibility, but a careful, intelligent approach should minimize this risk.

Sketching

Annotating a simple sketch can be a good way to quickly note down the details of a mystery bird. Your sketch does not need to be fine art – try using egg shapes to produce a basic bird shape. Learning some bird 'topography' can be useful too. While some of the more technical language may be off-putting at first, much of the labelling is pretty straightforward. Knowing your way around a bird will help you to describe a bird accurately and to understand the descriptions used in some field guides.

What is It Doing?

A bird's behaviour can provide very useful clues to its identity. If you see a roughly pigeon-sized bird hovering over a roadside verge in the UK, it is a Kestrel. How birds fly or walk can give clues too. Some birds fly in a straight line (e.g. Starling), others have an undulating flight (e.g. woodpeckers). Does it glide or flap its wings, or even alternate between the two?

Where is It?

While some birds are seen in many different habitats, others are more specific in their requirements. You would not expect to see a Puffin inland, for example. Not all the birds that occur in the UK are found in every part of the country – Ptarmigan and Capercaillie are only found in Scotland.

What Time of Year is It?

Some birds are residents – they spend the whole year in this country. Others are summer or winter visitors and spend the rest of the year somewhere else, and some birds just pass through when they are on migration (passage migrants). This information can help with identification.

Using Sounds

Bird songs and calls can provide excellent clues to help with identification. Do not leave learning songs and calls until you have got the hang of what birds look like – knowing some bird noises can make identification much easier and learning some songs and calls is not that difficult. Get to know some of the common birds first and take it from there. The descriptions of bird noises in books can be hard to interpret but using sound recordings can help, especially if you can take them out in the field with you. Alternatively, go bird-watching with a more experienced bird-watcher and learn from them or, when you hear a bird that you do not recognize, track it down and identify it visually too.

Some Tips

Get to know the local and common birds first and build your knowledge from there. Knowing the common birds well will help you to pick out the more unusual ones.

When faced with several species at once that you cannot identify, try to focus on just one of them. Some may 'get away' but you will gradually build your 'repertoire'. Try not to identify a bird on one feature alone. The 'safest' identifications are based on a range of different clues.

Expect to make some mistakes – it is part of the learning process. Stick at it and with time and application you will be the bird-watcher making those impressive split-second identifications!

What to Beware of

Birds that look similar are not always the same species – look at some of the pipits for example. To add to the challenge, some birds that look dissimilar are not different species! Males and females may look different (e.g. ducks, Blackbird), some birds wear their breeding plumage for part of the year only (e.g. Grebes, Black-headed Gull) and young birds can look different to adults (some gulls take four years to acquire their adult plumage).

Juvenile Birds

A bird's juvenile plumage is its first set of 'proper' feathers. For a short period of time, until at least some of the juvenile feathers are moulted, the young bird can look quite unlike its parents. You may still be able to detect the character of the species though, and the juveniles of some species look like

washed-out versions of the adults (e.g. Moorhen). One way to identify juveniles is to look for the adults who may be nearby.

Escapes

Not all birds seen in the wild are wild birds. Swans, ducks and geese escape from collections, and falconers and aviculturists lose birds sometimes. If you see a Black Swan it is unlikely to have made its way from the Antipodes!

Light Effects

The direction and intensity of the light can affect your perception of a bird's appearance. Colours may look different in different lights and a bird lit from behind may appear smaller than one lit from the front.

Abnormal Birds

Sooner or later you will see a bird that has some white feathers where it does not normally – a Blackbird with white wing feathers or white patches on the head for example. This is still a Blackbird, but for some reason, some of its feathers lack the normal black pigment. This is partial albinism – complete albinism is much more rare. Other birds may over-produce pigment. A melanistic bird is blacker or browner than normal. Abnormal pigmentation also produces other colour effects. Watch out for colour-dyed birds too – ornithologists may use a dye to mark a bird – to study the movements of swans or waders for example.

Not All 'Ducks' Are Ducks

To a beginner, Coots, Moorhens and Grebes may look like ducks. But when you search among the ducks in the field guide you won't find them. Most field guides are arranged in scientific order. All the ducks are together, but as these birds are not ducks you won't find them there. There is no easy solution to this apart from experience and leafing through your field guide in advance and familiarizing yourself with the birds you are likely to see.

Your Field Guide is exactly that – a Guide

Good-quality field guides are a great identification tool. But they are only a guide – not all of the birds you see will look *exactly* like the illustrations of that species in the book. But normally they are pretty close.

Other Bird-Watchers

Many bird-watchers are friendly and more than happy to assist with a 'tricky' identification. Take care though – the 'experts' that you meet are not always right. Try to work out that mystery bird for yourself too, don't just take someone else's word for it. You will learn more that way too.

Urban

and Surburban Species

Urban & Suburban Areas

Even the most densely populated urban areas can provide excellent opportunities for bird-watching. City centres may appear devoid of wildlife but they very seldom are. Pigeons, House Sparrows, starlings, swifts and martins are a familiar sight and are all birds that have adapted to live side by side with humans. Certain birds of prey are also utilizing our cities. The Peregrine Falcon is one such species. It is now a regular breeding bird in even the largest cities, using cathedrals and tower blocks to nest in place of its typical cliff- and quarry-face nest sites.

Varied Habitats

Green spaces within cities – parks, gardens and sports fields – open up other opportunities. Here can be found species such as tits, finches and thrushes. Gardens with well-stocked bird tables will usually have a plentiful array of birds. Winter can bring birds that would normally avoid urban areas into towns and cities in search of food. Ponds or boating lakes in parks should be checked during periods of harsh weather – as temperatures in urban areas are higher than in more rural areas, unusual species of duck and grebe may venture to these places if their normal haunts are frozen over.

Grass verges on main roads or railway embankments can also offer a green oasis in industrial environments. Such areas are often rich in flowers and consequently have a good selection of insects. This makes for some rich pickings for insectivorous birds such as warblers and chats.

Wasteland, although not particularly attractive, can also provide bountiful food sources for birds such as finches and buntings, particularly during winter when they can be found feeding on thistle heads and teasels.

Feral Pigeon

The Feral Pigeon is a truly urban bird. It is descended from the Rock Dove, a rare species restricted to coastal cliffs. It is a familiar resident of towns and cities, providing bird life in even the most built-up areas.

The Feral Pigeon has an incredibly varied plumage. Cross-breeding with domestic stock has led to an array of appearances. Essentially, however, the true Feral Pigeon has a blue-grey body with a greyer back. It normally has two black wing bars and a paler rump.

A Common Sight

It can be found literally anywhere where humans live – it is probably the most urban of all our resident bird species. The Feral Pigeon has adapted to breed in the most unlikely surroundings and can often rear young throughout the year. It will feed on a variety of seeds, but will also scavenge food waste.

The nest site is not grand and is usually sited on a ledge. A normal clutch consists of two white eggs.

Scientific Name:	Columba livia
Identifying Features:	Very variable plumage
Similar Species:	Rock Dove
Size:	31–34 cm (12¼–13 ⅜ in)
Habitat:	Towns and cities
Population:	Abundant

▶ Look more closely and you see the Feral Pigeon boasts a surprisingly attractive irridescence on its neck.

Wood Pigeon

The Wood Pigeon – a large, heavy pigeon and a gregarious feeder – is generally a bird of open country, where it is shot for food, but it has adapted well to life in the city. It is now a regular sight in town parks and gardens.

The Wood Pigeon is grey-brown above with a pale pink breast. It has distinctive white crescents or wing bars and a white and iridescent green patch on the neck. Sexes are alike but juveniles lack the neck patch, although the wing bar is present. Its call is a five-syllable 'coo'.

Into the City

Originally a farmland bird, the Wood Pigeon has now colonized most towns and cities where it can be found with relative ease. It breeds very early in the year – often as early as February – but this is dependent upon the availability of food.

Scientific Name:	Columba palumbus
Identifying Features:	White wing bar and neck patch
Similar Species:	Stock Dove
Size:	40–42 cm (15¾–16 ½ in)
Habitat:	Gardens, parkland
Population:	Common

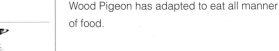

Grain and seeds are its natural diet but the Wood Pigeon has adapted to eat all manner of food.

Its nest is a thin, fragile-looking platform of twigs, where it lays one or two white eggs.

Collared Dove

The history of the Collared Dove is a rather short one. This bird originated from India, and spread across Europe. It arrived in Britain in the 1950s when a single pair bred. This rise continued for the next 20 years but has now eased off. Its rise has been nothing short of meteoric and can now be encountered in numerous habitats. The success of the Collared Dove can perhaps be attributed to its breeding season. Often three but sometimes as many as five or six broods can be raised each year by a single pair. It has a distinctive three-syllable call.

The Collared Dove is a pale, fawn-coloured bird with a pinkish breast tinge. The thin black collar on the neck is also a key feature. Its long tail has a prominent black bar with a white tip. The juvenile birds have a duller, paler plumage with no black collar. The Collared Dove has a distinctive display flight, which consists of a steep rise into the air before gliding down.

Habits

Collared Doves can be found in parks and gardens, although they are equally at home in more open country. They are quite adaptable and will frequent bird tables; many are very approachable.

The species has a prolonged and prolific breeding season. It can often raise multiple broods in a single year, and may keep the same partner for many seasons. It feeds on a range of grain, seeds and fruit. It will also take bread and scraps when natural food sources are scarce.

The Collared Dove's nest is a shallow and untidy platform made of twigs, usually situated near the trunk of a tree. The bird typically lays two white eggs.

Scientific Name:	Streptopelia decacto
Identifying Features:	Pinkish-buff plumage with thin, dark neck bar
Similar Species:	Turtle Dove
Size:	31–33 cm (12¼–13 in)
Habitat:	Gardens and parkland
Population:	Common

Swift

Often called 'The Devil Bird' because of its screaming call, the Swift is a common summer visitor. What is remarkable about this bird is its ability to spend large amounts of time in the air. Only when it is nesting does it come to land and roost normally. It is thought that a young Swift can spend the first two years of its life on the wing without ever landing.

Swifts have a dark, sooty plumage and although they appear black they are actually dark brown, often with a distinctive whitish throat and chin. Their profile in flight is also distinctive, with scythe-shaped and exceptionally long wings that arch backwards. They also have a shallow notched or forked tail, which gives greater control in flight. The loud screaming call is a common sound in towns during the summer months.

Breeding and Feeding Habits

Swifts are found in all urban habitats, choosing to nest in roof spaces and eaves. Churches, cathedrals and towers are also favoured locations. They demonstrate an interesting breeding pattern for an insectivorous bird, in that the young hatch at carefully staggered intervals. This is to ensure that in poor summers at least the first-hatched chick will survive, even if the subsequent nestlings do not.

Swifts eat an array of flying insects, including gnats and midges. They are thought to catch in excess of 10,000 insects each day, from around 300 different species.

The Swift's nest is a shallow cup of its own feathers and detritus, bound together by its saliva. Two or three eggs are typical per brood and these are creamy white.

Scientific Name:	Apus apus
Identifying Features:	All dark with scythe-shaped wings
Similar Species:	Swallow, House Martin
Size:	16–17 cm (6¼–6¾ in)
Habitat:	Towns and Cities
Population:	Common summer visitor

House Martin

Another summer visitor to towns and villages across Britain and Europe, the House Martin is smaller and daintier than the Swift, but just as agile in the air. It builds distinctive mud cup nests under the eaves of houses. During prolonged summer droughts its numbers may be fewer, as it is heavily reliant upon mud for the construction of its nest. Once the summer is over the House Martin returns to Africa, but exactly where it spends the winter months remains something of a mystery.

Adult House Martins have iridescent blue upperparts with darker wings. The underparts are white and they also have a distinctive white rump. The tail is quite short but with a small but noticeable fork at the tip.

Homes and Food

Originally, before the onset of human dwellings, the House Martin nested on cliffs. These days the majority of these birds reside in towns, cities and villages. They are summer visitors and should be looked for from May onwards. Towards the end of summer large numbers will gather on wires as they prepare for the migration back to Africa. They are not social nesters particularly, but often when there is more than one brood the earlier young will take on some of the parental care, feeding chicks from subsequent broods. House Martins feed on winged insects, taken in flight. The nest of the House Martin is largely constructed of mud and small amounts of plant material. This is generally positioned under the eaves of a roof with an opening at the top. The eggs are white and a typical clutch size is between four and five.

Scientific Name:	*Delichon urbica*
Identifying Features:	Distinctive white rump
Similar Species:	Swallow, Sand Martin
Size:	12 cm (4¾ in)
Habitat:	Towns and Cities
Population:	Common

Wren

The Wren is an active, tiny bird common throughout our region. In harsh winters this species is very susceptible to the cold and to help combat this they have communal roosts. These can sometimes number more than 50 birds in a single nest box or similar. The male Wren often creates more than one nest during the spring and whichever one the female chooses, and lines with feathers, is where the young will be raised that year.

This minute bird is a reddish-brown colour above with slightly paler barred underparts. It also has a noticeable cream-coloured eye stripe. Its short tail is often cocked and is a good feature to look for. The combination of the short tail and small head give the Wren a very rounded appearance. Its flight is generally fast, direct and very low to the ground. Its song is surprisingly loud for such a small bird and consists of a metallic rattle.

Habits and Habitat

The Wren can be found in a variety of habitats although parks, mature gardens and woodland are particular favourites. The male is often polygamous, having two or more mates. It can construct up to a dozen nests for the female, or females, to choose. If the male is monogamous then it will help to rear the young with the female. This is less common in polygamous birds. It is an insectivorous bird and feeds on spiders, ants, caterpillars, beetles and mites.

The nest site is usually low down in a tree crevice or situated in ivy or creepers. It is made of plant material and is domed. The female lays around five eggs, which are white with faint red mottling.

Scientific Name:	Troglodytes troglodytes
Identifying Features:	Tiny with tail often cocked
Similar Species:	Dunnock, Goldcrest
Size:	9–10 cm (3½–3⅞ in)
Habitat:	Gardens, parkland and woodland
Population:	Common

Dunnock

The Dunnock is an unremarkable bird to look at, its name derived from 'dun-coloured bird'. It is also occasionally referred to as the Hedge Sparrow, although it is not a member of the sparrow family at all but belongs to the Accentors. During the spring, look for males, often several in number, as they perform their wing-waving display. Despite its drab appearance and habits a male Dunnock can often attract multiple females, and three females in attendance is not uncommon.

Adult Dunnocks are a tawny-brown colour streaked with black. The head, with its darker face mask, and breast are a slate-grey colouring. There is also a paler wing bar, which is sometimes noticeable in flight. Juvenile birds are more heavily streaked with some mottling.

Mating and Nesting

Dunnocks will be found in most gardens, often visiting bird tables, but they also favour woodland settings. This is a bird that will often have multiple partners during a single breeding season. In these

instances an unusual feature of the Dunnock is that of stimulating a female using his bill. This is thought to encourage the female to eject sperm from any previous mating encounter, thus ensuring that he is the male to fertilize the eggs. The Dunnock has the slim bill associated with insect-eaters and will hunt for food under hedges and on lawns. However, it is quite capable of eating and digesting small seeds during the winter months when live food may be less plentiful. It creates a cup-shaped nest of leaves, grasses and roots, lined with softer material. It is usually found low down in a hedge or bush. It has four to five eggs, which are a vivid turquoise colour.

Scientific Name:	Prunella modularis
Identifying Features:	Brown upperparts with blue-grey underparts
Similar Species:	Wren, warblers
Size:	14 cm (5½ in)
Habitat:	Gardens, parkland and woodland
Population:	Common

Robin

The Robin is a familiar bird, which always seems to be associated with Christmas, although it can be seen year-round. Its striking red breast is incredibly distinctive but avoid confusion with the juvenile birds, which do not possess this colouring. The Robin will pair from early December and are one of the few birds that hold territory all year. They are fiercely territorial and males have been known to attack and, on occasion, kill other Robins that pose a threat.

A distinctive species that is apparently much loved amongst bird-watchers, both sexes share the red breast, bordered by pale blue-grey feathering. The upperparts are a dull olive brown. Younger birds tend to have a mottled breast turning to red after moult. During late summer adult birds undergo a post-breeding moult, during which time they can become extremely secretive and difficult to observe. Their song is a pleasant but mournful thrush-like warble and is often delivered in the dead of night.

Courtship

When protecting their territories, Robins will display their red breasts with vigour to any potential intruders. The female will chase the male during the breeding season until she is accepted. Once this has happened, the male Robin can be seen feeding the female as part of the courtship process.

The Robin is largely an insect-feeder but will also take earthworms. It will, however, take fruit and seeds and is fond of berry-bearing plants. The nest is made of leaves, moss and grass, and often a Robin will build a nest in sheds or outhouses. A typical clutch size is four or five eggs although six or seven is not uncommon. The eggs are creamy white spotted with red.

Scientific Name:	Erithacus rubecula
Identifying Features:	Distinctive red breast
Similar Species:	None

Size:	14 cm (5½ in)
Habitat:	Gardens, parkland and woodland
Population:	Common

Blackbird

The Blackbird is one of the best-known and best-loved city-dwelling birds and can be found with ease in most habitats. Only the male Blackbird is actually black, with a distinctive yellow bill and eye ring. Females are a mixture of browns. Watch for Blackbirds as they run along lawns, stopping with their head cocked to one side, as they search for earthworms. Although this creates the impression that they are listening for movement, they are in fact looking.

The unmistakeable adult male has jet-black plumage, although in flight the wings can appear somewhat paler. The female is much duller and has a mottled throat and breast. Young male Blackbirds are superficially similar to adult females. They have a dull bill that turns to the familiar yellow after the spring moult. They often retain the brownish wing feathers grown as nestlings until after the first full moult. Their song, which is usually delivered from a prominent position, consists of notes that are formed together into phrases.

Where to Look

Blackbirds can be found pretty much anywhere, and they are regular visitors to gardens. Although they will visit bird tables they are more likely to be found feeding on the ground, on lawns and in borders. Blackbirds

are quite territorial. Actual physical attacks on other males are rare but have been documented.

During the summer months they will eat a range of insects and worms. In winter they will eat seeds and berries. They build a tidy cup nest of mud and mosses, lining it with grass. The eggs are an attractive blue-green colour with brown speckles. There are often two broods, each consisting of four to six eggs.

Scientific Name:	Turdus merula
Identifying Features:	Male black with distinctive yellow bill
Similar Species:	Ring Ouzel
Size:	24–25 cm (9$\frac{1}{2}$–9$\frac{7}{8}$ in)
Habitat:	Gardens, parkland and woodland
Population:	Abundant

Song Thrush

The Song Thrush is an attractive speckled bird and a familiar sight, although in recent years it has undergone something of a decline. Snails form a large part of its diet and it will regularly use a rock or stone to break open the shells. These are referred to as 'anvils'.

Distinctive

The Song Thrush has warm brown upperparts but is paler underneath. The buff-coloured breast is covered in familiar black spots. It also has a distinctive orange underwing.

Its song is melodic and consists of a phrase of two or three notes repeated. Once common in gardens, the Song Thrush has undergone a decline in numbers. However, they can be found with relative ease in gardens and woodlands. As well as snails, they will feed on earthworms, a variety of insects, fallen fruit and berries. The nest is made of leaves and twigs and the Song Thrush lays four or five eggs, pale blue and spotted with black.

Scientific Name:	Turdus philomelos
Identifying Features:	Distinctive spotted breast and orange underwings
Similar Species:	Mistle Thrush, Redwing
Size:	23 cm (9 in)
Habitat:	Gardens, parkland and woodland
Population:	Common

▶ The Song Thrush has an attractive melodic song and is a joy to see in the garden.

Mistle Thrush

The Mistle Thrush has the old country name of 'Storm Cock'. This is largely due to its habit of singing from the tops of tall trees in the most inclement of weather. This bird is larger and noisier than the Song Thrush and has a noticeable white underwing.

The Larger Cousin

The Mistle Thrush is the largest of the resident thrushes. They are superficially similar to the Song Thrush but larger. The spotting on the breast is much heavier and they have a white underwing.

Although they will be seen in large, mature gardens they are more likely to be encountered in parks and woodland. It is a very early breeder, starting to attract a mate as early as December and often eggs can be laid in February. It will eat some insects but is particularly fond of fruit and berries.

Scientific Name:	Turdus viscivorus
Identifying Features:	Boldly spotted underparts and white underwing
Similar Species:	Song Thrush, Fieldfare
Size:	27 cm (10½ in)
Habitat:	Gardens, parkland and woodland
Population:	Common

The nest is rather untidy and is laid in the fork of a tree. Clutch size will be between three and five eggs and although the egg colour can be variable they are generally brown and speckled.

▶ As well as Storm Cock, another ancient country name for the Mistle Thrush is the Throstle.

Blue Tit

A charming, inquisitive member of the tit family, the Blue Tit is a welcome addition to any garden bird table. They are single-brooded and usually time their breeding to coincide with an abundance of their foodstuff – caterpillars. They can lay up to 15 eggs in this brood but if the food is not plentiful enough then there is no second brood. Installing a nest box will help attract Blue Tits to your garden all year round.

The Blue Tit is an attractively marked bird with a vivid blue cap, wings and tail. Its underparts are a bright, clean yellow in colour. The face is white with a noticeable darker eye stripe. Younger birds have greener caps with a yellow, rather than white, face. Its vocabulary is a mixture of thin, high-pitched churring calls.

History and Habitat

The Blue Tit began life as a woodland species but has adapted to more urban habitats. It is now a familiar sight in gardens as it visits bird tables in the winter and uses nest boxes. Blue Tits are prolific breeders and a brood in double figures is not unusual, as is the presence of a second brood during the season, should an adequate provision of food allow.

Caterpillars are the mainstay of a Blue Tit's diet. They are very active feeders and as they are so light they can seek food at the tips of the thinnest twigs, giving them quite an advantage. The Blue Tit is a hole-nester and as well as using nest boxes it will utilize holes in trees and buildings. Clutch size can be anything from seven to 15 eggs; these are white with reddish-brown spots.

Scientific Name:	Parus caeruleus
Identifying Features:	Yellow underparts; white cheek with black line through the eye
Similar Species:	Great Tit
Size:	11–12 cm (4¼–4¾ in)
Habitat:	Gardens, parkland and woodland
Population:	Common

Great Tit

The Great Tit is a larger, more boisterous relative of the Blue Tit, essentially another woodland bird that has adapted to be at home in parks and gardens. It is a very adaptable bird and is renowned for utilizing a large variety of unusual nest sites. It has one of the most varied vocabularies of all our birds and if you hear an unfamiliar call in your garden, there is a higher than average chance that it will be a Great Tit.

The adult Great Tit has a striking combination of white cheeks with a black crown and bib, and a bright yellow breast. It has a thick black band running vertically down the centre of its breast. The wings and tail are blue-grey in colour with the tail having prominent white outer feathers. Although both sexes possess the breast band it is noticeably broader on the male and unbroken, whereas it is much thinner on the female. It has an extremely varied voice with myriad calls, phrases and notes, although the song is a repetitive 'teacher, teacher, teacher'.

Feeding and Breeding

The Great Tit is a species that feeds largely on caterpillars but will also take seeds, fruit and peanuts. During the winter they regularly drop to the ground tossing aside leaf litter and moss as they search for food. Nest boxes are a favourite but they will often take advantage of man-made sites such as holes in pipework. Clutch sizes can be large but on average number five to seven. The eggs are white with red spotting. The male is another territorial species and the female is known to hiss at predators should they approach the nest site.

Scientific Name:	Parus major
Identifying Features:	Black cap, collar and throat with a black line running down the breast; white cheeks
Similar Species:	Blue Tit, Coal Tit
Size:	14 cm (5½ in)
Habitat:	Gardens, parkland and woodland
Population:	Common

Starling

The Starling is a familiar sight in urban areas. However, despite its relative abundance there are still many mysteries about this bird and more careful observation is needed. Although it may appear to be rather dull-looking, close-up it is actually a striking iridescent green with pale, whitish flecks. In winter the Starling is a communal rooster and will travel many kilometres to reach a favoured site. Often the number of birds in established roosts can reach tens of thousands.

At close quarters the Starling is really quite an attractive bird. During spring the male is a glossy mix of green and black with a distinctive yellow bill. At the base of the bill is a blue patch. This is pinkish on the female. After its autumnal moult the tips of the feathers are pale, giving a speckled appearance. Juvenile Starlings are a dull grey-brown with a dark bill. The song is not particularly grand – more a long mixture of rattles. However, the Starling is an exceptional mimic and can impersonate many other species as well as other sounds such as car alarms and telephones.

Eating and Nesting

This is another species that is often polygamous. Another interesting, but inexplicable, fact about this bird is that where a group of Starlings are nesting the egg-laying between the pairs will be synchronized so that they are all laid at the same time. Insects and their larvae are the preferred food of the Starling but it will eat largely anything, particularly in an urban setting.

They nest in holes and crevices in buildings and trees using a variety of materials. Research has shown that certain plants are chosen to line the nest. These possess some types of natural toxins to eliminate parasites. The eggs are pale blue and number between four and six per clutch.

Scientific Name:	Sturnus vulgaris
Identifying Features:	Blackish bird with green-blue sheen; heavy speckling
Similar Species:	Blackbird
Size:	21 cm (8¼ in)
Habitat:	Gardens, parkland and woodland
Population:	Abundant

House Sparrow

The House Sparrow has seen a decline in numbers in the last few years, although it is still quite abundant. It is an excellent example of humans living side by side with birds. It can be found in the most urban of areas and although largely sedentary, ringing recoveries have shown some individuals can travel in excess of 300 km (200 miles) away from their normal areas. The House Sparrow is easily recognized by its slate-grey cap and prominent black bib.

The male House Sparrow is quite distinctive, with a black bib, grey crown and grey rump. The wings are a mix of warm browns with a whitish wing bar. The female is drab by comparison – a rather nondescript greyish brown. The House Sparrow is quite a vocal bird but with a limited vocabulary of cheeps and twitters. They often congregate in large groups and the combined chattering can be quite a sound.

Humans and Sparrows

Most urban areas will have groups of House Sparrows. They are also present on farmland – in fact, wherever humans are, House Sparrows will follow. They are real opportunists and have managed to colonize the majority of the globe.

Essentially the breeding season is from May to July; however, there is an increasing tendency amongst this species to nest all year round, and three or four broods are not unusual. House Sparrows have a varied diet but strictly speaking they are seed-eaters. They will also readily eat berries and buds. In towns and cities, though, they will feed on scraps and discarded food waste. The nest is a rather untidy affair largely constructed of grass and straw. They will nest in holes or make loose nests in bushes. Three or four eggs are typical but a female can lay as many as seven. The eggs are greyish with fine darker speckles.

Scientific Name:	Passer domesticus
Identifying Features:	Slate-grey crown; distinctive black bib
Similar Species:	Tree Sparrow
Size:	14 cm (5½ in)
Habitat:	Gardens, parkland and woodland
Population:	Abundant

Chaffinch

The Chaffinch is probably the most common resident finch, and the male is a very attractive bird indeed. Although the resident population in Britain does not really wander, the winter sees the arrival of large numbers of Chaffinches from the continent moving in search of food. The Chaffinch builds an elaborate nest of grasses which it then decorates. For such a small bird they are long-lived and research has found individuals that have survived for 13 years.

There can be no mistaking the Chaffinch. The hand-some male has a pink breast with a blue-grey head that shows a noticeable peak. A double white wing bar is also evident, particularly in flight. Look also for the white outer tail feathers. The female is a much toned-down version of the male but can still show a faint pink wash to the breast. The female also has the distinctive white wing bars. In early spring the Chaffinch song can be heard – a short descending series of trills ending with a flourish. At other times it can be heard making a two-note chipping call, 'pink, pink'.

Habitat and Habits

Largely resident, this bird can be found in parks, gardens and open country as well. It is normally absent from very urban areas. The short, stubby bill tells us that the Chaffinch, in common with other finches, is a seed-eater but will take a range of other foods, including insects.

The Chaffinch pairs in late winter and is usually single-brooded. However, two broods are not uncommon. The nest of a Chaffinch is built low in a bush or tree, often in the fork of a branch. It is a cup nest that is lined with feathers and grasses. The exterior of the nest is usually decorated with lichens stripped from surrounding trees. The eggs are dark spotted and greenish. Four or five eggs is typical.

Scientific Name:	Fringilla coelebs
Identifying Features:	White shoulder stripe and wing patch; male has pinkish breast and cheeks
Similar Species:	Brambling, Bullfinch
Size:	14–15 cm (5½–5⅞ in)
Habitat:	Gardens, parkland and woodland
Population:	Common

Greenfinch

The Greenfinch is another easily found urban dweller. It is a fairly thickset finch with a characteristic undulating flight. These are increasingly familiar garden birds and are particularly partial to sunflower and niger seeds. They are solitary during the summer months but can form sizeable flocks during winter.

Colour in the Winter

As its name suggests, the Greenfinch is green in colour, although this is offset by yellow flashes in the wing and tail. The female is a little duller, streaked brown and with less vivid yellow colouration. The song is a mix of pleasant twittering notes.

Found in parks and gardens, especially during the winter months, it can also be encountered in a variety of other habitats such as woodland. Its diet is a wide range of seeds, berries and cereals.

Scientific Name:	Carduelis chloris
Identifying Features:	Olive-green with prominent yellow wing flashes Similar species:
Similar Species:	Siskin, Goldfinch, female Crossbill
Size:	15 cm (5⅞ in)
Habitat:	Gardens, parkland and woodland
Population:	Common

Greenfinches are aggressive birds during the breeding season, and they build nests of twigs and moss in bushes and hedges, laying four to six whitish speckled eggs.

▶ You are especially likely to find a Greenfinch during the winter months.

Goldfinch

Possibly the most colourful of all resident finches, the Goldfinch is a beautiful bird. It is less frequent in gardens than some species, but look for it on waste ground in winter. Here it will feed on its favourites of thistle heads and teasels.

Striking Features

The Goldfinch is slim built with a striking facial pattern of red, black and white. Prominent yellow wing flashes on black wings are another key feature. During the spring it can be seen with two brownish patches on each side of the otherwise pale breast.

Goldfinch song is a very liquid mix of twittering. The Goldfinch is another seed-eater, with a preference for members of the thistle family. They can be found occasionally in gardens but are more likely to frequent waste ground.

They build tidy cup nests, constructed of wool and mosses, usually at the end of a branch. Eggs are bluish with some streaking and spotting, usually numbering five or six.

Scientific Name:	Carduelis carduelis
Identifying Features:	Distinctive red, white and black face; yellow wing flashes
Similar Species:	Greenfinch, Siskin
Size:	12 cm (4¾ in)
Habitat:	Gardens, parkland and woodland
Population:	Common

▲ The Goldfinch was once a popular cage bird, trapped using a cage called a Chardonneret – its French name.

Bullfinch

The Bullfinch is a stout, dumpy finch with a reputation for doing vast damage in orchards, where it feeds on the buds of fruit trees. For a bird with such a vivid plumage the Bullfinch can often be secretive. The female is a toned-down version of the male in terms of plumage and they can often be encountered feeding in pairs. The noticeable white rump in flight is a good identification feature.

There can be few resident finches as striking as the Bullfinch. It is a plump, large-headed finch with a very short stubby bill. Its wings, tail and cap are all a glossy black in colour. The breast, underparts and cheeks of the male are a glorious rich pink. The female is nowhere near as colourful, with a pinkish-brown wash. The noticeable white rump is present in both sexes, as is a silvery white wing bar. Its song is a quiet warble, but is rarely heard.

A Secretive Species

The Bullfinch is an urban visitor during the winter months, but in the spring and summer it retreats to woodland or mature parkland to breed. During the winter its population is swollen by migrants from the continent.

In terms of breeding patterns the Bullfinch is unremarkable. Its secretive nature has made it difficult to study. One interesting fact, however, is that during the breeding season the adults develop a pouch within their mouths to carry food.

The staple foods of the Bullfinch are buds from a variety of trees. Oak and hawthorn are favoured, as are the buds of fruit trees. These preferences make the Bullfinch a pest species for commercial growers. It nests between May and July in flimsy-looking nests of twigs and mosses. Here the female will lay four to five bluish-green eggs.

Scientific Name:	Pyrrhula pyrrhula
Identifying Features:	Black cap and white rump; male has vivid pinkish underparts
Similar Species:	Chaffinch
Size:	14 cm (5½ in)
Habitat:	Gardens, parkland and woodland
Population:	Common

Woodland

Species

Woodland Species

Woodlands are fabulous places for birds. There are three main types of woodland areas: deciduous woodland, where the leaves fall during the winter; coniferous woodland made up predominately of firs and pines; and mixed woodland, which has a combination of the two.

Mature deciduous woods offer possibly the largest selection of birds, particularly during the spring and summer. Warblers often dominate but other species that make this their habitat include flycatchers, woodpeckers and finches. Early mornings are one of the best times for this particular habitat, as the birds are generally very active and vocal. The dawn chorus is a fabulous experience and will often test your knowledge of birdsong. One factor to be wary of, however, is that during the spring and summer the dense foliage and natural cover can make some species very difficult to see. During the autumn and winter months this becomes less of a problem, but there may be fewer species at this time of year.

Coniferous woodlands generally hold fewer species than deciduous woodlands. The newer coniferous plantations are worth visiting, though, particularly if there are clearings and rides. These areas are often home to pipits, flycatchers and chats. Several species of the tit family prefer a coniferous environment, as do Siskins and the crossbill family. Members of this last have adapted in a remarkable way to live in coniferous woodland. Their upper and lower mandibles have become crossed or twisted. Although this may look a little comical, it makes them more adept at removing seeds from fir cones than any other bird.

Sparrowhawk

In the 1950s the Sparrow-hawk was in trouble. Its numbers were seriously affected by the use of agricultural pest-control chemicals such as DDT. The more intensive the agriculture in a certain area the worse the problem became. With the tighter controls against these practices today, the Sparrowhawk is now quite common. As its name suggests, birds form largely the entire diet of this species. After killing its prey, the Sparrowhawk will often take it to a regular perch to be plucked.

Sparrowhawks are small and fast-flying birds of prey. The male has a slate-grey back with reddish barred underparts. The female is often considerably larger than the male and has browner upperparts and paler barred underparts. The female also has a characteristic white stripe above the eye. Both sexes have a series of four or five bars on the tail. Young birds have red-brown upperparts with some barring below. It is silent for most of the year but is known to make a shrill, four-syllable call when nesting.

Recovering Resident

Once heavily persecuted, the Sparrowhawk has made something of a recovery in recent years and is now a common resident. It can be seen in our gardens and parks as well as woodland and open country. It is another early nester and the display flight should be looked for in April.

The Sparrowhawk is a specialist of hunting smaller birds – not just sparrows, but also finches and tits. It has been known to take prey as large as a pigeon. A nest of twigs and sticks is made against the trunk of a tree, where the female lays four or five whitish eggs.

Scientific Name:	Accipter nissus
Identifying Features:	Rounded wings; speed in flight
Similar Species:	Goshawk, Kestrel
Size:	28–38 cm (11–15 in)
Habitat:	Gardens, parkland and woodland
Population:	Common

Tawny Owl

The Tawny Owl is the most common breeding owl. Originally a woodland species, it has adapted to life in parks and gardens. Given its strictly nocturnal nature, the Tawny Owl can be a difficult species to see. During the day its presence can be made known by the anxious chattering of other birds as they come across a roosting owl. These verbal attacks can be quite prolonged.

The Tawny Owl is a thickset owl with a large rounded head. It is reddish-brown in colour with noticeable white markings on the wings as well as on the crown. Around its face is a ring of darker feathers, creating what is called a facial disc. There is also a grey form of the Tawny Owl but these are not commonly recorded. Its call is a well-known hoot but it also has a sharp 'ke-wick' that can often be heard.

Nesting and Feeding

Deciduous woodland is where the Tawny Owl makes its home, although they are also found in large, mature gardens and parkland. The male is particularly territorial during the breeding season and they have been known to attack people should they feel a threat to the nest site.

The nest is made in the hole of a tree or in a nest box, although there have been instances of this species nesting on the ground. Eggs in a normal clutch number between two and five and are white.

Small mammals make up the main part of this species' diet, such as mice and voles. They also take small birds, beetles, frogs and earthworms. The Tawny Owl has even been recorded snatching fish from the surface of water.

Scientific Name:	Strix aluco
Identifying Features:	Largish owl; reddish-brown; well-rounded wings
Similar Species:	Long-eared Owl, Short-eared Owl
Size:	37–39 cm (14⅝–15⅜ in)
Habitat:	Gardens, parkland and woodland
Population:	Common

Green Woodpecker

Green Woodpeckers are the largest species of woodpeckers. Both sexes share the bright green plumage and red crown, but the red moustache stripe is only seen on the male. Once spotted it is largely unmistakable, with its vivid plumage and deep, undulating flight – a common characteristic of the woodpecker family. Ants and their larvae are the Green Woodpecker's main diet and the birds can often be seen plundering an ant hill.

This is a large and distinctive woodpecker. The upperparts are a dark green while the underparts are paler and greyer. The red crown is present in both sexes but the male also possesses a red moustachial streak, which is entirely black in the female. Juveniles are similar in plumage but tend to have heavy barring on the breast and flanks. The call is an easily recognized laughter-like call. They do not normally drum, like some woodpeckers, but when they do it is weak.

Where to Look

Green Woodpeckers can be found in deciduous woodland, parkland and open country, occasionally visiting gardens. Despite being a woodpecker, they will often feed away from trees in open grassy areas such as lawns, playing fields and open pasture.

When breeding the Green Woodpecker is particular about its nest site and quite precise on location. The nest is usually about 4 m (13 ft) above ground with an entrance hole no wider than 6 cm (2⅜ in). The nest chamber is then excavated to a depth of around 30 cm (11⅞ in). Ants, together with their eggs and larvae, are a large part of the Green Woodpecker's diet, as are beetles, flies and caterpillars. Mature trees, particularly oak and ash, are favoured. The nest chamber is lined with wood chippings and a typical clutch size is five to seven glossy white eggs.

Scientific Name:	Picus viridis
Identifying Features:	Predominately green plumage; red crown
Similar Species:	Golden Oriole
Size:	31–33 cm (12¼–13 in)
Habitat:	Woodland
Population:	Common

Great Spotted Woodpecker

Great Spotted Woodpeckers are usually found in deciduous and mixed woodland, but they are also a visitor to gardens. They have a distinctive pied plumage with flashes of red on the nape of the neck and base of the tail.

Useful Aids to Identification

The large and obvious white wing patches are a useful aid to identification in flight. Its drumming sound is a familiar noise in woodlands. It can be seen with regularity away from woodland haunts, where it travels to feed at garden bird tables.

Most of its natural food – a large variety of insects and their larvae, particularly beetle larvae – is obtained by repeated pecking of dead and decaying wood and bark.

Scientific Name:	Dendrocopus major
Identifying Features:	Black and white with red under-tail feathers
Similar Species:	Lesser Spotted Woodpecker
Size:	22–23 cm (8⅝–9 in)
Habitat:	Woodland
Population:	Common

Both sexes excavate a nest chamber and incubate between four and six white eggs in an unlined nest chamber.

▶ The Great Spotted Woodpecker has usefully distinctive white wing patches.

Blackcap

The Blackcap is also a summer visitor; however, increasing numbers of this species have adapted to overwinter here. The black cap that gives it its name can only be seen in the male. The female has a reddish-brown cap. For such a small warbler, the Blackcap can be surprisingly dominant and aggressive. Often when feeding the male will puff out its breast feathers to make it appear larger, although this is also an added protection against colder temperatures.

Slightly smaller than a House Sparrow, the Blackcap is a common sight in our woodlands. The male is grey-brown above with paler underparts. The distinctive black cap is only to be found on the male, in the female it is chestnut brown. Besides the cap colouring it is a rather ordinary-looking warbler. The juvenile is a duller version of the female. The song of the Blackcap is a pleasant melodic tune made up of rich, clear notes and generally ending with a flourish.

Food and Nests

It is common in our woodlands during the summer and many birds choose to overwinter here. During the winter they will often enter gardens in search of food. Summer food is made up of caterpillars, flies and beetles. During the winter, however, it will feed on fallen fruit, bread and other scraps from the bird table.

When breeding it is a very aggressive bird and will challenge rival males that enter its territory by puffing out its breast feathers and raising its cap. The male builds several nests. The female will choose a nest and then adapt it into a tidy, delicate cup-shaped nest. These can be found in dense vegetation such as brambles. It generally lays five eggs and they are creamy white with brown speckling.

Scientific Name:	Sylvia atricapilla
Identifying Features:	Noticeable black cap, brown in the female
Similar Species:	Garden Warbler, Marsh and Willow Tits
Size:	13 cm (5 in)
Habitat:	Woodland, parks and larger gardens
Population:	Common

Garden Warbler

This warbler is rather nondescript and has no obvious outstanding features. It is vaguely reminiscent of the Blackcap but without the coloured crown. However, it does possess a glorious song and rates as one of the most musical song birds. The song is quite quiet and mellow with long phrases punctuated with short silent intervals. It often stays on late in the season, adapting its largely insectivorous diet to take in the autumn crop of berries and small fruits.

The Garden Warbler is a dumpy, plain brown warbler with a short and stout bill. The upperparts are largely brown with paler underparts. As the breeding season progresses the adults tend to become greyer. Sexes are alike and the juveniles are similar to the adult birds, appearing more olive when the plumage is fresh. The song can be heard from April and is a mixture of musical phrases that is remarkably similar to the Blackcap, although the deliverance of the Garden Warbler's song is more sustained, often lasting in excess of a minute.

Warbling Insectivore

Despite its name, the Garden Warbler is rarely found in gardens, unless these are large and mature. It breeds in deciduous and mixed woodland where there is thick undergrowth to give cover. It can occasionally be found in open country where there are copses or hedgerows. The Garden Warbler is insectivorous and will eat most invertebrates. They are also known to eat berries and other fruits.

The male, like many in this family, builds a number of rudimentary, unfinished nests. They allow a female to choose and then she completes the finishing touches. The cup-shaped nest is built low down in a bush or hedge and constructed using grass, leaves and small twigs. Clutch size is usually five eggs and these are off-white with darker blotches.

Scientific Name:	Sylvia borin
Identifying Features:	Dull with no obvious features
Similar Species:	Blackcap, Chiffchaff
Size:	14 cm (5½ in)
Habitat:	Woodland
Population:	Common

Chiffchaff

Like the Blackcap, the Chiffchaff often overwinters in our region, although it is essentially a summer migrant. It is very similar to the Willow Warbler in appearance, but is generally not as brightly coloured and has darker legs. It arrives early and its familiar two-syllable call, from where it gets its name, can often be heard from March onwards. It can often be found feeding on the ground, particularly during spring and autumn passage and will repeatedly flick both its tail and wings.

The Chiffchaff is a familiar bird of our woodlands. Its upperparts are generally dull green or brownish with a contrasting pale rump. It also has a pale eye stripe. The underparts are a dull yellow. It is similar to the Willow Warbler, although it is a duller bird with dark legs, whereas the Willow Warbler's legs are pale. The species are, however, best separated by their songs. The song of the Chiffchaff is like its name, and this phrase is usually repeated three times.

An Early Nester

Chiffchaffs can be found in deciduous and mixed woodland, parks and some gardens. They are largely absent from coniferous woods. They feed mainly on insects, including midges and flies, but will occasionally take berries and seeds (although this is unusual).

The Chiffchaff is an early nester, from late April. The female builds a dome-shaped nest, low down in the undergrowth. Four to six eggs are typical – white with faint darker markings.

Scientific Name:	Phylloscopus collybita
Identifying Features:	Dull green upperparts; paler breast; dark legs
Similar Species:	Willow Warbler, Wood Warbler
Size:	11–12 cm (4¼–4¾ in)
Habitat:	Woodland, gardens and parks
Population:	Common summer visitor

Willow Warbler

The Willow Warbler is a close relative of the Chiffchaff and is a common summer visitor. They have a pleasant, tuneful descending song. They are very similar to Chiffchaffs but generally much cleaner in appearance and with flesh-coloured legs. However, there are many variations in both species and often the voice can be the only determinable feature. It feeds actively on insects and can often hover or dart out from a favourite perch, not unlike a flycatcher.

The Willow Warbler is a small, slim leaf warbler. It has green-brown upperparts but is noticeably pale yellow underneath. As the summer progresses this yellow will fade. It has pale legs and a dark line through the eye with a pale yellow stripe above. These are features to help distinguish the Willow Warbler from the Chiffchaff. Willow Warblers are also noticeably longer winged. Their song is a liquid series of notes ending with a pronounced flourish.

Variety of Habitats

Willow Warblers can be found in a variety of habitats, including deciduous and mixed woodland. They are also found in open country, especially where there are hedgerows. They are becoming increasingly urban and can be found in large gardens. Their diet is a range of insects including flies, caterpillars and beetles. They will also eat berries and similar fruits, particularly in the autumn.

Some male Willow Warblers are polygamous. They normally have one brood per year but the polygamous males will often raise a second brood with a different female. The Willow Warbler usually nests on the ground in a delicate domed nest, with an entrance at the side. The nest is constructed from grasses and moss. There are between four and eight eggs and these are white with reddish-brown speckles.

Scientific Name:	Phylloscopus trochilus
Identifying Features:	Greenish-brown upperparts; yellowish underparts
Similar Species:	Chiffchaff, Wood Warbler
Size:	11–12 cm (4¼–4¾ in)
Habitat:	Woodland and parks
Population:	Common summer visitor

Goldcrest

The Goldcrest, along with the Firecrest, is our smallest bird, measuring in the region of 9 cm (3½ in). It is a tiny but very active bird with a striking orange or yellow crest which it raises when agitated. In can be found in all types of woodland, although it prefers to nest in conifers. It creates a cup nest usually suspended from a branch. Goldcrests can often be seen during the winter months in the company of other birds, such as tits, in large mixed flocks.

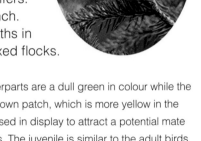

This minute bird is rather round-looking with short wings. The upperparts are a dull green in colour while the underparts are pale off-white. The male has a distinctive orange crown patch, which is more yellow in the female (from where it gets it name). The crown patch, or crest, is used in display to attract a potential mate and ward off any intruders. There are also two faint white wing bars. The juvenile is similar to the adult birds but without the crown patch. Both song and call are a high-pitched series of notes.

Diverse Habitats

The Goldcrest can be found in a range of different habitats. Woodland, scrub, gardens, parks and churchyards all attract this species. It feeds almost exclusively on insects, such as flies and caterpillars, and spiders. Occasionally it will also take small seeds.

When it comes to the breeding season the Goldcrest will favour coniferous woodland and plantations. The nest is an ornate cup of mosses, lichens and spiders' webs. The nest is suspended from each end and it is built towards the end of a branch. The Goldcrest will lay up to eight eggs, which are white with faint spotting.

Scientific Name:	Regulus regulus
Identifying Features:	Active bird with yellow or orange crown stripe
Similar Species:	Firecrest
Size:	9 cm (3½ in)
Habitat:	Coniferous woodland, large gardens
Population:	Common

Spotted Flycatcher

The Spotted Flycatcher is the most common member of this family. It is heavily reliant on insect prey and often arrives late when there is an abundance of its food. Spotted Flycatchers do not feed entirely on insects and the female will often take woodlice and snails. It is thought that this is to ingest calcium to strengthen eggs.

This is a plain, but rather nicely patterned flycatcher. The upperparts are grey-brown in colour while the underparts are off-white with noticeable streaking. The wings have pale edges to the feathers. Both the wings and tail are quite long and the bill is dark and broad at the base. Sexes are alike and the juvenile is a mottled, blotched version of the adult. The call is said to resemble a squeaky handcart, while the song is a quite melodic but high-pitched scratchy warble.

Feeding and Migratory Habits

Spotted Flycatchers have declined in recent years but can still be found in deciduous and mixed woodland. They are also found in mature gardens, parkland and particularly churchyards. As its name implies, this species hunts flying insects, usually from a prominent post or perch. It will dart out, catch its prey and often return to the same perch to start again. During less clement weather it will search among leaves to find aphids and caterpillars. Cold, damp weather in May and June will curtail its feeding activities and it may well abandon breeding for that season.

Most Spotted Flycatchers arrive in May to breed, which makes it one of the last migrants to arrive. It is a long-distance migrant and starts its return journey as early as July, unless it is double brooded in a particular season. It is also a nocturnal migrant, choosing to fly only at night. It nests on ledges or open-fronted nest boxes. Very often it will nest using ivy as a cover. The nest is a cup nest, loosely assembled using twigs and grasses. The eggs are white with pale red blotches and usually number between four and five.

Scientific Name:	Muscicapa striata
Identifying Features:	Grey-brown with streaking on a paler breast
Similar Species:	Dunnock, Tree Pipit
Size:	14–15 cm (5½–5⅞ in)
Habitat:	Woodland, parks and gardens
Population:	Common

Long-tailed Tit

Despite its name and similar appearance the Long-tailed Tit is not actually a member of the tit family. It belongs to the babblers, a group not often encountered in our region. It is quite unmistakeable, with its extremely long tail and distinctive plumage. Often during the winter large flocks of Long-tailed Tits can be seen, sometimes 20 or 30 in number.

Aptly Named

The Long-tailed Tit is a small and dumpy bird with a remarkably long tail – over two-thirds of its body length is its tail. It is a pinkish brown above and paler below, with a pinkish tinge. The head is largely white but with distinct black lines above the eyes. There are pink and white patched on an otherwise dark wing.

Sexes are similar. Their song is rarely heard but is an extension of its high-pitched calls. The birds can be found along deciduous woodland edges and also in parkland and gardens.

Scientific Name:	Aegithalos caudatus
Identifying Features:	Extremely long tail; attractive black, white and pink plumage
Similar Species:	Pied Wagtail
Size:	14 cm (5½ in)
Habitat:	Woodland
Population:	Common

It feeds on flies, beetles, caterpillars and a range of other invertebrates. Its nest is an elaborate oval construction made with moss and leaves, then bound with spiders' webs. Eggs will number between eight and 12 and are white, spotted red.

Coal Tit

Although the Coal Tit can be seen in deciduous woodland, its home is really coniferous woodlands and pine plantations. It is a rather dumpy and short-tailed tit but extremely agile and acrobatic when feeding. The males and females of the species are identical but juvenile birds can usually be identified by their more yellow plumage. Coal Tits have a distinctive single-syllable call that often gives its presence away in thick, dark pine woodland.

The Smaller Cousin

The Coal Tit is smaller than the Great Tit, with similar black head markings and white cheeks. It lacks any yellow plumage and is a dull bluish-grey above with paler buff underparts.

The characteristic white nape is distinctive. They can be found breeding in coniferous woodland but at other times of the year can be encountered elsewhere, including gardens. They feed mainly on insect larvae but during the winter will eat seeds and peanuts from bird-table feeders.

Another hole-nester, Coal Tits tend to nest low to the ground. They lay between seven and 10 red-spotted white eggs.

Scientific Name:	Parus ater
Identifying Features:	Black head with white cheek patches and nape
Similar Species:	Great Tit, Crested Tit
Size:	11–12 cm (4¼–4¾ in)
Habitat:	Woodland, often coniferous
Population:	Common

▲ Coal tits can be separated from others of the family by the distinctive white nape.

Nuthatch

Nuthatches are dumpy, rather solid-looking little woodland birds. They possess long thick bills to enable them to break open acorns and beech mast. They are hole-nesters but do not excavate their own; they use a ready-made site and then proceed to plaster the rim of the entrance hole

with mud. This is done to prevent larger predators entering the nest cavity. Its black eye stripe is a distinctive feature when seen at close quarters.

The Nuthatch is a fairly common woodland bird, roughly the size of a Great Tit but resembling a diminutive woodpecker. The bill is dark and dagger-like, and there is a distinctive black stripe through the eye. Upperparts are blue-grey while it has paler underparts. The lower flanks are a rich chestnut colour. Sexes are similar and the juveniles resemble the adult birds but with less chestnut colouration on the flanks. Their call is a loud 'tewit, tewit, tewit, tewit', which increases in intensity when alarmed.

Habitat, Nests and Eggs

Nuthatches can be found in deciduous woodland, parkland and large, mature gardens. They are rarely seen in coniferous woodland but will venture into mixed woodland to feed on fir cones during the second half of the year.

Despite its name, during the spring, the Nuthatch feeds on a range of invertebrates including beetles and spiders. During the autumn and winter months it will feed on the nuts and fruits of acorns, hazel, beech mast and similar. It is a hole-nester, but adopts old nests rather than excavating its own. Occasionally it will use a nest box. The females lay on average six to 10 eggs which are white with pale red markings.

Scientific Name:	Sitta europaea
Identifying Features:	Blue-grey above with pinkish underparts
Similar Species:	Blue Tit, Great Tit
Size:	14 cm (5½ in)
Habitat:	Woodland
Population:	Common

Treecreeper

The Treecreeper is a small and delicate mouse-like bird with a thin down-curved bill. It uses this bill to probe tree bark for insects and aphids. It can often be watched as it spirals and winds up the length of a tree. It very rarely climbs downwards, preferring to leave the tree and start at the base of another nearby. It nests in cracks in trees or behind pieces of loose bark.

The Treecreeper's upperparts are barred brown with paler streaks. It has a noticeable pale stripe above the eye. Underparts are white and it has a brown rump. The tail feathers are long and pointed. In flight the pale wing bar is often noticeable. Sexes are similar and the juvenile is difficult to distinguish from the adult birds. Its voice is a high-pitched two-syllable call, and its song is a high-pitched warble. In fact, the songs and call of the Treecreeper are so high-pitched it can be difficult for humans to hear.

Broods

The Treecreeper makes its home in deciduous and coniferous woodland. It can also be found in copses, parks and gardens. In the winter it may also be seen in open country where there are mature hedgerows. It will eat insects of most kinds and during the autumn and winter will also eat small seeds, particularly those from pines and spruce.

The Treecreeper is generally single-brooded, however, research has shown that pairs nesting in coniferous woodland often raise a second brood. They nest in a cavity, usually behind ivy; the nest is lined with small twigs and plant material before being finished with moss and spiders' webs. They lay between four and eight red-spotted eggs.

Scientific Name:	Certhia familiaris
Identifying Features:	Mouse-like with obvious curved bill
Similar Species:	None
Size:	12–13 cm (4¾–5 in)
Habitat:	Woodland
Population:	Common

Jay

The Jay is an attractive member of the crow family, or corvids. It is well marked with salmon-pink colouration, iridescent blue feathering in the wing and a distinctive crest. Despite its handsome appearance the Jay can be incredibly wary and secretive. Listen for its unusual cat-like call. Jays can be encountered with more regularity in autumn as they forage for acorns, one of their staple foods. They will often collect these in large numbers and stash them away by burying them, retrieving them during the winter.

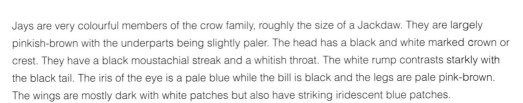

Jays are very colourful members of the crow family, roughly the size of a Jackdaw. They are largely pinkish-brown with the underparts being slightly paler. The head has a black and white marked crown or crest. They have a black moustachial streak and a whitish throat. The white rump contrasts starkly with the black tail. The iris of the eye is a pale blue while the bill is black and the legs are pale pink-brown. The wings are mostly dark with white patches but also have striking iridescent blue patches.

Habitat

They favour deciduous woodland, particularly oak. They can be incredibly secretive during the breeding season and are often heard rather than seen. During the autumn months they become more obvious as they forage for acorns. The Jay adores these nuts, although they will also take beech mast and other fruits. Like other members of the crow family they will also take eggs and nestlings of other birds.

The nest of twigs is built by both birds in a tree or shrub. Jay eggs are a pale blue-green or olive with darker blotches. A typical clutch size is between four and five.

Scientific Name:	Garrulus glandarius
Identifying Features:	Pinkish brown with blue, black and white wings
Similar Species:	None

Size:	34 cm (13⅜ in)
Habitat:	Woodland
Population:	Common

Jackdaw

Jackdaws are members of the crow family and have the uniform black plumage associated with these birds. When seen at close quarters the beady pale eye is one of their most distinguishing features. They are quite long legged and walk with a peculiar gait. They are noisy birds and can often be quite aggressive. They nest, often in large groups, in old trees. However, they are becoming increasingly urban and can be found in towns and villages where they nest on buildings, often using old chimney pots.

The Jackdaw is a small crow that appears all black from a distance; up close, however, they have a grey neck and pale eyes. Most of the plumage is black or a silvery greyish black except for the cheeks, nape and neck. These are light grey to silver. The iris of adults is greyish white and is quite noticeable at close range. The sexes are similar but juvenile birds show a pale blue iris rather than grey. The call is a harsh 'tchak, tchak'.

Sociable Breeders

They are found in both coniferous and decidous woodland, as well as open country, towns, villages and more urban areas. The bird is a sociable breeder, nesting in often large colonies. Pairs of Jackdaws will often stay together for several years. They usually nest in colonies in cavities of trees, cliffs or ruined and sometimes inhabited buildings, usually in chimneys, and sometimes in dense conifers. The eggs usually number four to five and are a pale blue-green in colour.

Jackdaws are largely ground-feeders, where they eat insects and other invertebrates. They will also eat seeds and grain and when in an urban environment, will eat scraps.

Scientific Name:	Corvus monedula
Identifying Features:	Black but with silvery sheen to the nape
Similar Species:	Carrion Crow, Rook
Size:	33 cm (13 in)
Habitat:	Woodland; occasionally urban areas
Population:	Common

Open Country
Species

Open Country Species

'Open country' is a blanket term for a number of British habitats, each with its own set of birds. It includes the broad spectrum of different farming habitats, plus rough grassland, heath, moorland and scrub. In such places are some of our most familiar birds, such as the Skylark, the Pheasant, the Carrion Crow and the Swallow.

On the whole, open country, by definition, suggests a lack of trees, and this has several implications for the bird community. Many species live primarily on the ground, or among deep cover, and this means that, when the time comes to attract a mate, they have to be very obvious or very noisy – or both. Thus the Skylark leaves the ground to make itself heard and seen on its marvellous song-flight, while the Common Whitethroat leaves the brambles to do the same, although on a more modest scale.

Other spectacular visible courtship displays are made by the Montagu's Harrier, the Lapwing and both the Meadow and the Tree Pipit, while such birds as Quail, Red-legged Partridge, Corncrake and Nightjar make astonishing and far-carrying sounds, often at night.

Interestingly, birds of open areas usually have higher-pitched songs than woodland birds. High-pitched sound quickly dissipates in leaves, so the birds sing lower pitches to compensate. Thus the Skylark or the Meadow Pipit might have difficulty making themselves heard in more enclosed habitats.

Most of the birds of this section will be found on farmland, but some are more specialized. The Dartford Warbler, Woodlark, Great Grey Shrike and Nightjar, for example, are typical birds of lowland heath, while the Corncrake requires damp meadows and the Grasshopper Warbler low scrub. Naturally, there are plenty of birds that also intrude into other habitats, such as crows and Magpies into towns, but they are at heart open country birds, and are treated as such here.

Red-legged Partridge

Introduced into Britain in the eighteenth century from the Continent, the Red-legged Partridge has found this country thoroughly to its liking ever since, recently leaving the native Grey Partridge far behind in terms of population. It is less slavishly a ground bird than the Grey Partridge, and sometimes surprises observers by sitting on roofs, gateposts and haystacks. It is even possible to imagine that it once perched in the branches of a pear tree, giving rise to the famous Christmas song.

If you should ever hear what seems to be the puffing sound of a steam-engine in the middle of a field at sunset, the chances are you will actually be listening to the territorial call of a Red-legged Partridge. This extraordinary performance is delivered by the male to proclaim rights to a patch of land. If an intruder threatens, the territory-holder will stand upright, puff out its white throat, raise its colourful flank feathers and, in a state of high dudgeon, make frenetic half-circles around its visitor.

Flocks and Breeding

This non-native Partridge is a common bird of slightly more open, less grassy habitats than the Grey Partridge, but is still a regular sight flying off on rapid wing-beats across open fields. In common with most game birds, it is sociable outside the breeding season, sometimes gathering into flocks of 50 or more. These flocks forage mainly on seeds, roots and leaves, which they unearth from bare ground using the bill, rather than the feet as in most of their relatives.

The Red-legged Partridge shows an unusual breeding quirk. Although many pairs bring up young together, a female will sometimes lay two clutches of eggs, one for herself to incubate, and the other for her mate. Each adult is then responsible for the welfare of their resulting chicks, although the two halves of the family may meet up again in midsummer.

Scientific Name:	Alectoris rufa
Identifying Features:	Short tail; red legs; white throat, black necklace; black on flank stripes
Similar Species:	Grey Partridge, female Common Pheasant
Size:	32–34 cm (12⅝–13⅜ in)
Habitat:	Open country and farmland
Population:	Common

Pheasant

The true home of the Pheasant is East Asia, but it has managed to settle with great ease into the foreign fields of both Europe and North America. True, its populations are maintained by annual releases for hunting purposes, but it is likely that, even without this somewhat dubious help, it would still be a common, albeit incongruous, feature of the landscape. It is really so familiar, indeed, that it is easy to overlook the male's quite astonishingly colourful, spangled plumage, topped by its superb, elegant long tail.

Not that the female is particularly interested in the complexities of the plumage. What marks the best males out for her is the extent of the red wattles on the male's face, which inflate slightly when the bird is excited. The male will show its intent, too, with some delightful, courteous displays, one of which involves circling the female and spreading its slightly open wings on the ground in front of her.

A Territorial Bird

Male Pheasants are highly territorial, and seldom aim to attract just one female to their patch of ground; instead, they work hard to acquire a small harem which, very occasionally, may number 10 or more females, but usually two or three. These females lay eight or more eggs each, in what can be a very productive season for a successful male. On the down side, however, some males cannot acquire a territory at all, and spend a frustrating season harassing paired females.

After breeding, male and female Pheasants often gather into single-sex flocks and spend their time scratching with their feet for grain, seeds, roots and snails, or using their bills to dig and pick. At night they roost up in the trees, often giving loud calls prior to settling down, which are slightly strangled versions of the familiar coughing crow.

Scientific Name:	Phasianus colchicus
Identifying Features:	Male unmistakeable; sometimes has white ring round neck; female has longer tail than other game birds
Similar Species:	Partridge, Red and Black Grouse
Size:	53–89 cm (21–35 in) of which tail up to 47 cm (18½ in)
Habitat:	Mainly farmland and woodland edge; edges of marshes
Population:	Common

Red Kite

It is the Red Kite, not the kite with a string, that came first. The toy was named after one of Britain and Europe's masters of the air – a bird that can change direction with the mere twitch of its unusual forked tail, or dive down with a flick of the wings. The Red Kite's history is as up and down as any aerial manoeuvre it might perform: once common as a scavenger in London and other big cities, it was persecuted to near extinction by the beginning of the twentieth century, before a strong, conservation-driven recovery in recent years, aided by the introduction of birds brought from the Continent.

Despite its reputation as a scavenger, a bird that once frequented the gallows in medieval times and now frequents rubbish dumps and even bird tables, the Red Kite is also a well-adapted predator. In the spring, especially, it is perfectly capable of snatching living food such as voles and other small mammals, and even the occasional bird. It uses a quick pounce, striking feet first, and thus tends to surprise its victims.

Red Kites build a nest of sticks at a modest height in a tree, often in a traditional site used down the generations. They sometimes betray their status as scavengers by adding such adornments as rags, plastic bags, dung and sheep's wool to the structure; even under-wear has been recorded!

The young, of which there are between one and three, hatch after 31 days into these moderately insalubrious surroundings and, in contrast to the situation in some birds of prey, grow up without murderous sibling aggression. One bird that does excite the Kite's ire however, is the Carrion Crow. Crows sometimes attack Kite nests and the Kites respond in kind, while at a good feeding site the two species constantly bicker over corpses, with much thieving and counter-thieving.

Scientific Name:	Milvus milvus
Identifying Features:	Pale grey head; forked swallow-like tail
Similar Species:	Buzzard, Marsh Harrier (at a distance)
Size:	60–66 cm (23⅝–26 in)
Habitat:	Farmland, sheep country; breeds in woodland
Population:	Once very rare, can now be locally common

Buzzard

Much the commonest large bird of prey in Britain, the Buzzard is also the most confusing. It shows a bewildering variety in its plumage, with some birds all-dark and others pale and creamy, depending on the individual. Little is consistent, except the broad wings, with 'fingers' at the tip, and the Buzzard's short tail. Thus it is a species that often leaves even experienced bird-watchers with red faces.

It is almost as unpredictable in its feeding habits. Although a large bird, with a presumably healthy appetite, it is as likely to be seen wandering over ploughed fields in search of worms as it is to be pouncing from a height on to a young rabbit, or some other favourite delicacy. A catholic diet is the norm, with voles nevertheless a consistent feature, together with carrion from roadkills and a few larger, more cumbersome birds such as Wood Pigeons or crows. The Buzzard can sometimes be seen hovering, or at least 'hanging in the air', while homing in on prey below. Typically, it will also perch upon fences and roadside poles, looking more like a surveyor of traffic than a voracious predator.

Nesting Habits

Buzzards are more territorial than other birds of prey and are reluctant to allow others within their borders, so it is a common sight to see quite a number of these birds in the air at once, circling at their invisible boundaries. They are also more vocal than other raptors, uttering a marvellous wild mewing call. Pairs are relatively sedentary, remaining in the territory throughout the course of the year. In the breeding season they build a substantial nest out of sticks and twigs, which is typically lined with fresh green material, possibly as a sort of chemical disinfectant to keep away parasites. Up to four young may fledge from successful nests.

Scientific Name:	Buteo buteo
Identifying Features:	Short tail; often pale 'necklace'; soars with wings in shallow V
Similar Species:	Honey Buzzard
Size:	51–57 cm (20–22⅜ in)
Habitat:	Upland and lowland farmland or moorland with nearby woodland or crags
Population:	Common and widespread

Kestrel

You cannot separate the Kestrel from its distinctive mode of hunting. This is the bird so often seen hovering over the verges of motorways and other major roads, or over agricultural fields, moorland or wasteland. Although it does hunt in others ways, for example sitting on a high perch (such as a telegraph pole or wire) and dropping down on to prey, it is never so easy to see as when it is hanging in the air, flying into the wind with wings steadily beating and its head absolutely still.

The main food of the Kestrel is small mammals, especially voles. Voles are diurnal, but the Kestrel will also hunt at dusk and dawn for mice, and has also been recorded hovering by moonlight. Interestingly, recent research has shown that this small raptor is able to see in the ultraviolet spectrum, which is bad news for voles, because their urine has an ultraviolet component. Since the voles use urine for scent marking and rarely go for long without relieving themselves, this enables the Kestrel to use urine-trail density to assess the abundance of voles in a particular area.

Early Courtship

For Kestrels, living in open areas, it is often a problem to find a suitable nest site, and this certainly limits its abundance. Nests are usually located in holes in trees, buildings or cliffs, while the birds also take readily to open-fronted nest boxes. Another major nest site is in the abandoned nests of birds such as crows, and this reflects the fact that Kestrels do not make any significant structure of their own. The most DIY they attempt is to make a shallow scrape for the four to six eggs.

The breeding cycle, however, begins long before eggs are laid. Males may start displaying to females as early as February, two to three months in advance; they plunge from a height towards the female and veer away at the last moment, and otherwise show off their aerobatic skills.

Scientific Name:	Falco tinnunculus
Identifying Features:	Easiest to identify by its hovering habit; long tail; narrow, pointed wings
Similar Species:	Hobby, Peregrine, Merlin
Size:	32–35 cm (12⅝–13¾ in)
Habitat:	Open country
Population:	Common but declining

Lapwing

The Lapwing is no ordinary wader. For one thing, it does not like wading or getting its feet wet. It is not even particularly fond of water, often being found well inland on agricultural fields and pasture, where it feeds in large flocks on earthworms, leatherjackets, caterpillars and ants. And for another, it looks unlike any other related bird. Not only does it have glistening iridescence on its upperparts, which glints spectacularly in the sun, but it also has peculiarly broad, rounded wings, which are beaten in a slow, lazy manner, quite unlike the usual powerful, fast wing-beats of other waders.

In spring and early summer, those unusual wings are put to good use during the Lapwing's sensational courtship routine. The male takes to the air and immediately flaps its wings with unusually deep beats, gaining height in what is known as the 'butterfly flight'; it will then make a series of ascents and steep plunges, often lurching from side to side, apparently out of control, and even flipping briefly over on to its back. This wild flying is accompanied by equally excited yelps, like a child on a rollercoaster, together with strange tearing and whooping sounds, and the wings, for their part, add in a loud throbbing.

Mating Displays

Further, more subtle displays take place on the ground. A bird of either sex settles down and scrapes away dirt with its feet. This is a prelude to nest building. The four eggs are laid in a small depression made in the same way, and the female sits tight for a month before they hatch. During this time, both parents often become highly agitated as one after another, various intruders going about their business are harassed by the noisy birds. Harmless cows and sheep, as well as crows and birds of prey, are subjected to mock attacks and overwrought squeals.

Scientific Name:	Vanellus vanellus
Identifying Features:	Iridescent green above with purple tints, white below; toffee-coloured undertail; wispy crest
Similar Species:	None
Size:	28–31 cm (11–12¼ in)
Habitat:	Agricultural fields, marshes, coastal mudflats
Population:	Common

Stock Dove

Few birds are so overlooked or under-appreciated as the Stock Dove, a very classy and attractive bird of woodland and farmland. It is smaller and less cumbersome than the similar Woodpigeon, with a more intense ash-grey colour to the body, and a vivid iridescent neck-ring lacking the adjacent white patch. It flies with faster wing-beats than the Woodpigeon and looks more compact. It is rarely seen in large numbers, and is thus much less of an agricultural pest than its irrepressible relative. Furthermore, Stock Doves feed on a wider range of vegetation than their relatives, taking seeds, shoots and leaves from many different types of plants, not just crops.

Another distinction from other pigeons and doves is that the Stock Dove usually makes its nest – such as it is, which is not more than a few twigs at most – inside a hole in a tree. Sometimes it will use a hole in a cliff or wall instead, but essentially the Stock Dove is limited to places where suitable holes are found adjacent to short-grass turf and pasture land, where the birds forage. In common with other pigeons, the Stock Dove lays two white eggs, and the young are fed for their first few days on 'pigeon milk', a rich, paste-like substance formed in the crop.

Stock Dove Call

These birds can breed almost throughout the year, but they can be very unobtrusive. In contrast to the Woodpigeon's loud, insistent song, for example, Stock Doves merely utter a soft, repeated, somewhat questioning coo, which is easily drowned out by the chorus of birds and other woodland sounds. In addition, their flight display is also distinctly understated; pairs of birds simply fly around in a wide circle, sometimes daringly raising their wings in a shallow V as they do so. The whole performance, as so much about the Stock Dove, is easily missed.

Scientific Name:	Columba oenas
Identifying Features:	Dark eyes, short tail; plum-pink breast; iridescent neck mark
Similar Species:	Woodpigeon, Feral Pigeon
Size:	32–34 cm (12⅝–13⅜ in)
Habitat:	Open woodland, farmland, cliffs
Population:	Common

Barn Owl

The pale, ghostly shape of the Barn Owl, most often seen as it hunts silently over fields at dusk, has excited much fear and suspicion among country-dwellers in the past, especially when the bird has uttered its typical rasping shriek – a sound to make the blood run cold in the semi-darkness. But in truth this bird poses no threat to humankind. Instead it is a ruthless and efficient hunter of small mammals, such as rats, mice and shrews, often doing a farmer a considerable service by nesting in an outbuilding or barn and keeping mammal numbers down.

The Barn Owl looks quite unlike other owls, with its peculiar heart-shaped face and small, black eyes. The arrangement reflects how it uses its senses. The eyes are only of secondary importance in hunting; it is the ears that hold sway. The facial discs help to amplify sounds, while the silent flight, typical of all owls, keeps background noise to a minimum. Internally, the ears are not symmetrical; the left is higher on the skull than the right. This means that sound travelling from below or above will arrive at one ear before the other, and this difference helps to compute the direction from which the sound is coming. In short, the Barn Owl has three-dimensional hearing. It is able to catch food in complete darkness.

Selecting a Mate

Barn Owls breed not just in barns, but also in churches and other buildings, as well as natural sites such as caves and tree holes. There is no real nest, the female just lays the four to seven eggs on the floor, often among old discarded owl pellets. The young hatch out after about 30 days, and then it will be another three months at least before they are independent. Interestingly, recent research has shown that males prefer to breed with females with plenty of spots on their thighs, an individual feature that appears to reflect a bird's state of health.

Scientific Name:	Tyto alba
Identifying Features:	Pale plumage; heart-shaped face
Similar Species:	Other owls will look similar in silhouette, especially in flight
Size:	33–35 cm (13–13¾ in)
Habitat:	Farmland, marshes and grassland
Population:	Fairly common

Skylark

There can be few more famous songsters than the Skylark, a bird commemorated in great music and literature for its sweet-sounding outpourings. And indeed, there are fewer more vivid experiences than walking in the countryside and being drenched in lark song for hour after hour. To deliver its song the male rises from the ground in a slow, hovering flight, and once it has reached its preferred height, often 30 m (100 ft) or more in the air, it will seemingly hang there, fluttering, as the song reaches its zenith.

In common with many great songsters, the Skylark is not very impressive to look at. It is surprisingly large, approaching the Starling in bulk, and, apart from its pert crest, has little to distinguish it. Of course, being bold and colourful is something of a liability for a bird that, like the Skylark, is mainly terrestrial and needs to be unobtrusive. It feeds on the ground, on insects and seeds, and also makes its nest there, a shallow depression lined with grass. The young are produced in a hurry; incubation lasts a mere 11 days, and the youngsters leave the nest before they can fly properly. All of this is designed to keep the most vulnerable stages to a minimum.

Winter Visitor

Many people think that Skylarks are only found in Britain in the summer, but this is not the case. The birds are resident, and large numbers of visitors actually come from the Continent to spend the winter season on our damp, relatively frost-free island. Most of the time they keep a low profile, feeding and roosting on the ground, often in flocks. But occasionally, on a mild winter's day, the odd bird is encouraged to sing, in readiness for the warmer season ahead.

Scientific Name:	Alauda arvensis
Identifying Features:	Distinctive hover; white trailing edge to the wings and white outer tail feathers
Similar Species:	Other small brown birds
Size:	18–19 cm (7–7$\frac{1}{2}$ in)
Habitat:	Farmland, grassland, coastal areas
Population:	Common

Swallow

There can be few more famous and popular birds than the Swallow. With an empire encompassing much of the world, it is welcomed as an incoming migrant wherever it goes, be it to the Northern Hemisphere (Eurasia and North America) in summer, or the Southern Hemisphere for the rest of the year. Everywhere it goes it lives in close association with people, feeding over fields grazed by livestock, and nesting on man-made structures, often on the eaves of barns.

With its long tail and swept-back wings, the Swallow is a master of the skies. However, in contrast to Swifts and most other members of its family, it usually hunts low down, zooming just above ground and having to dodge large animals by side-flips; this enables it to catch larger prey than other similar aerial birds, notably blowflies and horseflies, those pests of summer. With the Swallow's wide gape, it might seem as though it could simply fly along with its mouth open and snatch what it needs, but in fact every catch is made by sight, and carefully targeted.

Social Interaction

Swallows either breed as single pairs or in colonies, although the latter are small by the standards of their family. Within either system their social relationships are particularly fascinating. Experiments have shown that, within the population, some males have longer tails than others, and some pairs of streamers at the ends of the tail are of equal length, and others not. Females, it seems, prefer both length and symmetry in tails, and males so blessed acquire a mate rapidly. They are also favourites for copulation outside the pair bond.

The Swallow nest is a cup, lined with feathers or hay but made primarily out of mud pellets, sometimes a thousand or more. This need for fresh mud means these birds are usually found near a ready water source.

Scientific Name:	Hirundo rustica
Identifying Features:	Long tail-streamers; royal blue upperparts and breast-band, with red-brown throat; creamy belly
Similar Species:	Swift, House Martin, Sand Martin

Size:	17–19 cm (6¾–7½ in)
Habitat:	Open country, including farmland and villages, usually near livestock and water
Population:	Abundant summer visitor

Meadow Pipit

It might look small and feeble, but the Meadow Pipit is a tough bird. It is one of the few species that occurs on bleak uplands, moorlands, chilly fields and coasts throughout the year, eking out a living by eating small seeds and insects. It often rises from the feet with an air of complete panic, flying this way and that, shouting out 'tsip, tsip!', seemingly unable to decide what to do. On the ground it can look equally gormless, just wandering around aimlessly.

In the spring, however, the male Meadow Pipit performs a flight-song similar to that of the Tree Pipit, with the same parachuting finish. The display does, however, go on for longer, and the song is more monotonous than the Tree Pipit's, repeating a single note incessantly in the manner of a modern-style alarm clock. Its purpose is to defend a territory from other Pipits, as well as to attract a mate; both of these essential tasks are difficult to do while on the ground, and Meadow Pipits tend to occur in places without many elevated perches.

Dangers of Ground-nesting

Breeding can be perilous. The ground nest is vulnerable to predators such as weasels, crows and snakes, but this bird also has the added worry of attracting the attention of a Cuckoo. It is one of the Cuckoo's favourite hosts in Britain, and the larger bird will often home in on the Pipit's nest by monitoring the alarm reaction of the parents, which tend to become more and more agitated the closer the parasite gets. The Meadow Pipit should lay three to five eggs, which hatch after about two weeks, the young fledging after another 10–14 days. Some may raise three broods in a season.

Scientific Name:	Anthus pratensis
Identifying Features:	Pink legs; small, thin bill; heavily streaked down belly to flanks
Similar Species:	Tree Pipit, Rock Pipit
Size:	14.5 cm (5⅝ in)
Habitat:	Open country
Population:	Very common

Whinchat

To most British bird-watchers the Whinchat is far less familiar than its relative the Stonechat, especially with its tendency to occur in wilder habitats, such as bracken-covered moorland, and to be present for less of the year. So it is exciting when this bird's prominent pale eyebrow gives away its identity, especially on migration when Whinchats can turn up almost anywhere, well away from their favourite haunts.

In contrast to Stonechats, Whinchats are exclusively summer visitors, arriving in April and departing from August onwards. They are long-distance migrants, travelling all the way to tropical Africa for the winter, while Stonechats move within the country, or stay put close to their breeding grounds. Interestingly, the Whinchat has longer wings than the Stonechat, since these are more energy-efficient for extended flights.

Breeding Territory

Once it has arrived the male Whinchat sings a somewhat scratchy, fitful song full of imitations of nearby birds, and it sometimes embellishes its performance with a brief up-and-down song-flight. Males are extremely territorial, and quarrels between them are common. Their patches of ground, where they feed on insects gathered on brief excursions from an elevated perch, are very important to them. The bonds between male and female are not very strong, and last for a single brood at best, rather than a whole season.

The nest is placed on the ground, usually among long grass or bracken, plants that typify Whinchat country, and while Stonechats almost always seem to have gorse in their breeding territory, despite their name ('whin' is an alternative name for gorse) Whinchats often do not. The female lays four to seven eggs and when these hatch, unattached birds sometimes help the pair in feeding the youngsters.

Scientific Name:	*Saxicola rubetra*
Identifying Features:	Broad white/buff supercilium, white-edged tail
Similar Species:	Stonechat
Size:	12.5 cm (4⅞ in)
Habitat:	Rough grassy areas, usually with bracken, including moorland
Population:	Fairly common summer visitor, common passage migrant

Stonechat

This is the sort to delight bird-watchers, with its habit of perching in full view of observers for minutes on end, making itself easy to see and admire. The habit comes from its foraging technique. It feeds on invertebrates that move across patches of open ground, or fly through the air nearby; by sitting still it can watch for movement, and then fly suddenly to snap up whatever morsel it has spotted. The technique is similar to that of the Robin, although the Stonechat rarely perches on spades.

The Stonechat is a bird of various kinds of open country, anywhere where suitable perches are readily available. While the closely-related Whinchat can sit comfortably on the thinnest stems, including rushes and bracken, the Stonechat prefers more secure watch points, such as treetops, posts and gorse bushes. Although it is probably commonest of heathland, it is also drawn to coastal sites, including the rough ground above cliffs.

Call and Meaning

Even if the Stonechat were not conspicuous, it would still be an easy bird to find, simply because it cannot keep its mouth shut. It has a distinctive call, 'sweet-sack!', the latter half of which sounds vaguely like two small stones being tapped together. Recent studies have shown that the 'sweet!' part of the call is a code to any nearby young to keep their heads down. Meanwhile, the male has a pleasing if slightly strained song

which, if the bird is in a flamboyant mood, is given in a brief display flight.

The Stonechat nest is an untidy cup of grass and leaves placed on the ground, usually under a gorse bush. The young are turned out at almost factory speed, with broods overlapping so that, while the previous youngsters are still not independent, the male feeds these while the female is already incubating the next batch of eggs.

Scientific Name:	Saxicola torquata
Identifying Features:	Small, dumpy bird with a habit of standing upright and staying still on low perches
Similar Species:	Whinchat

Size:	12.5 cm (4⅞ in)
Habitat:	Open country, typically with gorse, especially heathland
Population:	Common resident

Fieldfare

Much as the first Swallow is a sign of spring, so the arrival of Fieldfares, usually in October, heralds the impending winter. These large thrushes arrive in Britain every autumn in enormous numbers from Scandinavia and north-central Europe, where they are abundant breeding birds, and they remain here until March or April. As they move about nomadically, they fly in characteristically loose flocks, intermittently giving distinctive 'shack-shack' calls, the sound of the season.

Fieldfares are closely related to our other thrushes, such as the Mistle Thrush, but they are highly distinctive to look at, with a tasteful combination of grey on the back and head, velvet back and black tail. The 'spots' you see on the breast are actually chevrons and arrowheads. These birds are almost always seen in loose flocks, usually moving over open ground on the lookout for soil invertebrates such as worms and leatherjackets, hopping a little and then standing still, watching around them, before pecking and digging into the soil. When they first arrive most Fieldfares are actually on the lookout for the autumnal crop of berries, which they gobble down with alacrity. Their favourite types are the larger ones such as sloes and rowan, although they also take haws.

Territorial Defence

Although Fieldfares are peripheral breeding birds in Britain, with minute numbers, they do have a very interesting and surprising aspect to their breeding biology. Nesting in large groups, the adults in a neighbourhood often club together when their colony is under threat from some predator such as a Hooded Crow. They all take to the air and, one after the other, bombard the intruder, pelting it with well-aimed excreta. A few minutes of such rough treatment soon moves the chastened predator on, sometimes with seriously soiled plumage. A few attacks can be fatal and, not surprisingly, the vicinity of Fieldfare colonies is an unusually safe place for other unrelated birds to place their own nests.

Scientific Name:	Turdus pilaris
Identifying Features:	Smoky-grey on rump, lower back and head; black tail; chestnut back; yellow bill
Similar Species:	Mistle Thrush, Song Thrush, Redwing
Size:	25.5 cm (10 in)
Habitat:	Scrubby country, hedgerows, fields
Population:	Abundant winter visitor

Redwing

Often referred to collectively with Fieldfares as 'winter thrushes', Redwings move in the autumn from Scandinavia to spend the cold season in Britain, where frosts are brief, snow is rare and the berry crop is excellent. In common with Fieldfares they live a nomadic lifestyle, moving across the countryside in informal flocks, checking out the hedgerows and damp field corners for food. In contrast to Fieldfares, Redwings also commonly enter woodlands to feed, where they search the leaf-litter for invertebrates.

The Redwing resembles a Song Thrush but is easily distinguished by its striking head pattern and, given a decent view, also by the eponymous leak of brownish-red under the wing. It also gives a distinctive piercing 'tsee' call when flushed, a sound that can also be heard when the birds are travelling about. They usually do this on still nights and, in the darkness, intermittent calls can give their presence away up in the sky above rooftop height, unseen. These birds are great travellers, and individual birds that spend one season here may well go elsewhere the next, to Spain or Greece, for example.

Taiga Bird

Although a very small number of Redwings breed in Scotland, this thrush generally has a more northerly range than its co-traveller the Fieldfare, essentially inhabiting the taiga forest belt of Northern Eurasia. Here it eschews forming large colonies itself, but will often nest next to Fieldfare colonies for safety. It builds a cup-nest in typical neat thrush style, and will often bring up two broods in a season.

Male Redwings have a curious singing quirk. Each individual sings just one phrase, repeated again and again; males in the same area share the same song. For a thrush, a family renowned for singing excellence and variety, this is rather surprising.

Scientific Name:	Turdus iliacus
Identifying Features:	Broad pale supercilium and pale stripe below ear-coverts; rusty-red flanks and underwing
Similar Species:	Song Thrush
Size:	21 cm (8¼ in)
Habitat:	Scrubby country, hedgerows, fields, woodland edge
Population:	Common winter visitor

Common Whitethroat

The Common White-throat is a perky, effervescent species of low, thorny scrub and copious undergrowth. Here it lives a fairly skulking life from April to September, picking insects and spiders off leaves and occasionally indulging in the odd berry, especially in late summer.

It would be hard to see were it not for its curiosity, and its need to perform its short, scratchy song. The latter is delivered either from a perch, sometimes a high perch such as an overhead wire, or during a brief display flight, in which the bird hovers in the air, rising and falling slightly. In the spring this song is performed almost all day long.

A Choice of Nests

Common Whitethroats nest low down in dense vegetation, sometimes among nettles. The male builds several nest structures, from which the female selects one to refurbish for breeding, and then she lays four or five eggs. These hatch after nine to twelve days and, once they leave the nest, the brood may be split so that each bird is responsible for feeding its allotted young.

Scientific Name:	Sylvia communis
Identifying Features:	Chestnut-brown panel on wing; dull pinkish underparts except for brilliant white throat
Similar Species:	Lesser Whitethroat, Garden Warbler, Blackcap
Size:	14 cm (5½ in)
Habitat:	Low scrub, hedgerows
Population:	Common summer visitor

▶ Common Whitethroats deliver their song from a perch or perhaps during a display flight.

Magpie

Everyone knows the Magpie, one of Europe's most familiar birds. But not everybody likes it. It has a reputation for thieving, which is based on myth. It has a reputation as a merciless killer of young birds and eggs in the garden, which is wildly overstated to the point of prejudice. It also has a mischievous chattering call and a pushy, wide-boy personality which undoubtedly grates with Middle England. But really, it is just a successful, opportunistic omnivore and deserves a bit of admiration.

Magpie society is quite complicated. It consists of two classes, one consisting of territory-holding pairs, the other of non-breeding birds that live in loose flocks. Every Magpie aspires to be a territory holder, because it is only these birds that can breed; the rest must wait for a vacancy, or try to sneak in by force. If you see a large, noisy gathering of Magpies assembled during the day, a fight over territory could be taking place, with one or more flock members challenging established birds. At night-time, Magpies also may gather in groups to roost in thick scrub, sometimes with the two classes mixing.

Spotting Magpie Nests

You can assess the abundance of Magpies in the area by waiting until winter and counting the distinctive domed stick-nests, usually placed quite high in a small tree. These nests are complicated structures, carefully interwoven and with a mud cup in the middle. The pair often begin building, or refurbishment, in the dead of winter. The birds only attempt to bring up one brood a year, and the clutch varies a lot in size, from only three to a challenging nine, the latter only attempted by experienced birds.

It is primarily when their young hatch that Magpies may predate the eggs or nestlings of smaller birds. It is a highly seasonal and peripheral activity, and they do not kill adults; but their reputation seems fixed in stone.

Scientific Name:	Pica pica
Identifying Features:	Black and white with long tail; black on wing; iridescent sheen
Similar Species:	None
Size:	44–46 cm (17³⁄₈–18 in)
Habitat:	Suburbs, farmland, woodland edge
Population:	Very common

Rook

It is often said that if you see a flock of crows they are Rooks and, while this is not quite accurate, there is little doubt that the Rook is by far the more sociable of these large black birds. For one thing, it nests in colonies, known as Rookeries, while crows nest singly. It also tends to feed in large flocks, which may cover whole fields as each bird digs around in the soil for invertebrates such as worms and beetle larvae.

The Rook is one of the earliest of our birds to nest in the spring, fitting in some nest-building before the turn of the year, and reaching the stage of incubating eggs by the middle of March. This is helped by the fact that immature birds tend to pair up in the autumn, while the adult pairs stay together for life. The stick-nests, placed high in trees, are a familiar part of the rural landscape, especially in winter when the leaves are absent and the stick platforms are most obvious. Once the residents have settled in, however, they are equally impossible to overlook, since the birds are forever coming and going from the feeding areas, and they are extremely noisy, making a wide range of caws and higher pitched sounds, the latter resembling the breaking of an adolescent voice. The commuting of Rooks between their nests and feeding areas in the spring, undertaken by direct flights, is almost certain to be the origin of the term 'as the crow flies'.

Brooding

Rooks attempt just one brood a year, the eggs hatching at a time when the chicks' main diet, worms, is abundant in the damp spring soil. Each female lays between two and five eggs and, although Rook partners pair for life, these eggs may carry the genetic matter of more than one male. Rape is a common fact of life in Rookeries, and the birds seem to be predisposed to some promiscuity anyway.

Scientific Name:	Corvus frugilegus
Identifying Features:	Bare, dirty white bill and face; steep forehead
Similar Species:	Carrion Crow, Jackdaw, Raven, Chough
Size:	44–46 cm (17⅜–18 in)
Habitat:	Farmland, towns
Population:	Common

Carrion Crow

Being clad in black all over and having the word 'carrion' in your name is not ideal for a positive image. And indeed, this crow is one of our least popular birds: farmers allege that it harms livestock, and gardeners shoo it from the bird table, claiming that it scares more attractive birds away.

A Bad Rep

There is little substance in either claim, but the crow is immune to all this anyway, and is a hugely successful bird, occurring in almost any habitat. It has a catholic diet which can include some live animals, plenty of dead meat and everything from scraps to fruit and berries.

In contrast to Rooks, Carrion Crows nest as single pairs, usually high in a tree, but also atop a cliff or building. The nest is a surprisingly complex structure, with at least four layers of different sticks and mud.

Scientific Name:	Corvus corone
Identifying Features:	Feathered face; dark bill; flat crown
Similar Species:	Rook, Raven, Jackdaw
Size:	45–47 cm (17¾–18½ in)
Habitat:	Diverse
Population:	Abundant

Crows raise up to seven young, and as the nestlings grow the nest can be a noisy place indeed: high-pitched croaks are quickly added to the adults' irritable cawing.

Linnet

Linnets in books always look spectacular, tending to show off the male's brilliant crimson breast and forehead, contrasting pleasingly with its grey head and warm-brown mantle. The reality, though, is that this bright colour scheme is only worn for a comparatively short part of the spring and summer, and for the rest of the year Linnets look like rather dowdy, small brown birds. They are, however, highly effervescent, sociable and talkative, so what they lack in colour they make up for in character.

Most bird-watchers come across Linnets in flocks, usually feeding in a corner of a weedy field. They do not feed in trees, nor even in bushes, but instead cling to stems or seed-heads, or stay on the ground. This bird's exceptionally short, stubby bill is adapted for taking very small seeds, especially those of weeds such as charlock, dock, mustard and buttercups, as well as oil-seed rape.

Nesting

The Linnet was once commonly kept as a cage-bird, on account of its pleasant, cheery demeanour and, especially, its song. The latter is a rambling affair, often delivered somewhat fitfully; but when it really gets going it is a wild, pacey, very varied and musical set of trills, a real delight.

Linnets often nest earlier in the year than other finches, from April, mainly because their favoured seeds are available before those favoured by other species – thistles for Goldfinches, for example. The structure is often placed in a thick bush, such as gorse, and tends to be lower down than most finch nests, sometimes even on the ground. Although many pairs nest alone, it is quite usual for three or four to use the same clump of bushes. Such birds often go on joint seed-hunting expeditions.

Scientific Name:	Carduelis cannabina
Identifying Features:	Longish, forked tail with white edges; white wing-panel; pale patches on face
Similar Species:	Redpoll, Twite, Greenfinch
Size:	13.5 cm (5¼ in)
Habitat:	Open country with bushes
Population:	Common

Yellowhammer

A few years ago almost everyone would have known the song of the Yellowhammer, encapsulated in the phrase 'A little bit of bread and no cheese'. Nowadays, however, the bird is no longer found at the corner of every field, and its favourite hedgerow habitat has been so drastically reduced that the declining Yellowhammer has faded from cultural consciousness, along with its dry, repetitive phrase. Its brilliant plumage, adorning bush-tops throughout the year, is also now an increasingly unusual sight.

The marvellous yellow plumage of the male in spring would, you might think, be wholly adequate to attract a mate; but in fact it is not the yellow, but the small red patches on the face that make the difference. The amount of red reflects the health and strength of the male, a measure of its ability to manufacture pigments from the seeds in its diet. Meanwhile, the song is a territorial tool to keep other males at a distance. It is sung quite incessantly, sometimes as often as 7,000 times a day, and for a long part of the year, right into midsummer and beyond.

Well-defended Territories

Yellowhammer nests are almost always built on the ground, the most typical site being at the base of a hedge, often on a slight bank. It is a well-hidden cup of grass and hay sprinkled with moss, into which the female lays between three and five eggs. Yellowhammers, like many ground-nesting birds, do not allow much time in the nest to their chicks, who leave after just 10 days or so, before they can adequately fly.

After breeding, the well-defended territories break down, and the birds become much more sociable. They often form flocks, although the membership is not fixed and individuals wander freely in search of grain and weed seeds. In the autumn the plumage is not so bright as in spring, and many people mistakenly think that Yellowhammers are summer visitors.

Scientific Name:	Emberiza citrinella
Identifying Features:	Male very distinctive and yellow, especially around head; female not as bright, but yellow wash usually obvious. Both have chestnut rump
Similar Species:	Cirl Bunting
Size:	16–16.5 cm (6¼–6½ in)
Habitat:	Farmland with hedgerows, grassland, scrub
Population:	Widespread and common

Freshwater &

Marshland

Species

Freshwater & Marshland

Wetland habitats – freshwater marshes, rivers, streams and lakes, and the range of associated bogs, swamps and reedbeds – are amongst the most productive of all places for birds, holding the greatest variety of species of any habitat. This is because water really is the stuff of life, supporting a wide range of insects and other invertebrates, fish, crustaceans and other items suitable as prey for birds of all shapes and sizes.

The most obvious birds of freshwater and marshland habitats are water birds, of which the majority of species are from the order Anseriformes – the ducks, geese and swans. These have evolved to exploit a wide range of different water levels and types of watercourse: from shallow water (dabbling ducks, swans) to deep water (diving ducks). But not every water bird you see is from this group: other groups, including divers, grebes, and two members of the rail family – Moorhen and Coot – are also represented.

Long-legged wading birds also love marshy areas: from the herons, egrets and bitterns, to members of the various wader families such as plovers and sandpipers.

Amongst such a range of water birds, it is easy to overlook members of other bird groups, not normally associated with water, that find their home here. Some songbirds have adapted to a more watery existence: notably the Dipper, which has become truly aquatic. Other songbirds, from warblers to buntings and the Bearded Tit to the Sand Martin, are also associated closely with water. And who could forget the monarch of all the water birds: the dazzling, orange and electric-blue Kingfisher?

So if you want to enjoy close-up views of some fascinating and varied species, and watch their behaviour at close hand, head for your nearest wetland – whatever the time of year, and whatever the location, you will not be disappointed.

Mute Swan

Britain's largest bird is also one of its best-known and best-loved. Long associated with the royal family, Mute Swans are often supposed to be owned by the Queen, though in fact this only applies to some birds. They are also legendary for their aggressive nature, with many urban myths suggesting that they are able to break a man's arm! In fact, although male swans will vigorously defend their territory they are unlikely to do much more than hiss at you.

Our only resident swan, the Mute Swan can be easily told apart from its two relatives, Whooper and Bewick's Swans, by virtue of the orange, rather than yellow, colour of its bill. Mute Swans also have a prominent black knob on the front of their bill – slightly larger in the male than the female.

Ugly Ducklings

Youngsters – the proverbial ugly ducklings – are grey when they first fledge, gradually acquiring their snow-white adult plumage during their first year of life. Mute Swans are found over most of lowland Britain and Europe, including many offshore islands. They will colonize a wide range of freshwater habitats.

Well known for their habit of pairing for life, swans build a large nest out of sticks, and lay up to eight eggs, which often become stained by vegetation during incubation, which lasts up to six weeks. The young swim immediately, and stay with their parents for several months afterwards.

Mute Swans feed by dabbling or ducking their head underneath the water, to pick up aquatic vegetation – they also occasionally take animals such as frogs and worms. They were once under threat from lead weights used by anglers, but following a ban populations are now well on the way to recovery.

Scientific Name:	Cygnus olor
Identifying Features:	Large, white; orange and black bill
Similar Species:	Whooper and Bewick's Swans
Size:	140–160 cm (55–63 in)
Habitat:	Rivers, lakes and ponds
Population:	Common

Canada Goose

Celebrated as a long-distance migrant in its native North America, the Canada Goose has a much less romantic reputation on this side of the Atlantic, having grown to pest proportions since it was originally introduced here more than two centuries ago. Brought to Britain and Europe by aristocratic landowners to decorate the lakes of their stately homes, its large size and aggressive habits have enabled it to spread throughout our cities, towns and countryside.

One of the easiest geese to identify thanks to its large size, and distinctive dark neck and head with contrasting white patch running from the base of the neck across each cheek. Birds occasionally hybridize with other geese, but their facial pattern is usually dominant enough for the observer to tell the parentage.

Wild Geese

Canada Geese are found on most kinds of waterway, from rivers and lakes to large park ponds and freshwater marshes, throughout lowland England and Wales and in parts of southern Scotland.

They are resident, although each autumn a handful of truly wild Canada Geese – often of one of the smaller, more compact races – cross the Atlantic and can be seen at locations in the north and west. These genuinely wild birds are much more wary of humans than their feral cousins, and usually associate with other wild geese such as Greenland White-fronts.

Canada Geese build a large nest out of leaves, grass and reeds, usually on the ground within easy reach of water – often on small islands where they can be safe from ground predators such as foxes. The young are, like many goslings, covered in yellowish-brown down, and fledge after about six or seven weeks. Like most geese, they feed mainly on plants.

Scientific Name:	Branta canadensis
Identifying Features:	Large size; pale belly; dark neck and head with white face-patch
Similar Species:	None
Size:	Size: 90–100 cm (35³⁄₈–39³⁄₈ in)
Habitat:	Lakes, rivers and marshes
Population:	Common

Mandarin Duck

One of the world's most striking and beautiful birds, the Mandarin Duck was, like several other exotic species of wildfowl, brought to Britain from its native China to provide ornament for stately homes. This tree-nesting duck has found the temperate woodlands of parts of southern Britain to its liking, and a small but well-established population continues to thrive in various parts of the country, including the London suburbs.

The male Mandarin

Duck is, quite simply, unmistakeable. No other bird boasts the same combination of features: the colourful head pattern and bright orange-red bill; the delicate feathering on the sides of the neck and, most striking of all, the two orange 'sails' poking up from the bird's back. Females are much less conspicuous – as befits their status as main parent at the nest. Nevertheless, their combination of contrasting greyish-brown speckled with white creates a very pleasing appearance.

Habitat and Breeding

Mandarin Ducks prefer large, tree-lined lakes – often favourite destinations for recreation – yet are often quite wary of humans. They frequently seek out the cover of waterside vegetation, only flying when flushed unexpectedly from their hiding place.

They nest in holes in trees, sometimes as much as 10 or even 15 m (33–50 ft) above the ground, from which the young must jump soon after hatching. Like so many hole-nesting species, the eggs are white, and are incubated for four weeks. The young remain with the parents until fledging about six weeks later.

Scientific Name:	Aix galericulata
Identifying Features:	Bright colours and orange 'sails' on male; greyish plumage speckled with white on female.
Similar Species:	Feral Wood Duck (North American)
Size:	41–49 cm (16–19 in)
Habitat:	Lakes fringed with dense trees and shrubs.
Population:	Scarce

Teal

Our smallest dabbling duck, the Teal is a favourite among birders for its diminutive size, beautifully marked plumage and secretive habits. It is often found in habitats where other ducks do not venture, such as tiny marshy pools and the edges of reedbeds, where small flocks can feed without being disturbed. Uniquely for a common bird, the Teal has never been known by any other name. The word itself has been adopted by interior decorators and fashion designers to refer to the rich, bluish-green colour of the patch running behind the male's eyes.

No other dabbling duck, apart from the Garganey, even approaches the Teal in smallness of size, which is often the easiest way to identify the species even at a distance, especially when it is associating with other ducks. Seen at closer range, the male's deep orange-brown head, contrasting with the bluish-green patch running from the eye to the back of the nape, are distinctive. Males also show a pale, yellowish stripe along their sides, and a noticeable yellow patch beneath the tail. Females are typically much less distinctive: basically speckled browns and buffs, with a darker cap and green speculum.

Habitat and Feeding

Outside the breeding season, Teal can be seen on a wide range of water courses, including large reservoirs as well as the smallest pool. When breeding they prefer to seek out thick cover to conceal their nest and eggs.

Teal feed by using several methods: on water they skim the surface or pick up tiny items of plant and animal matter; they also paddle slowly through shallow water or mud, filtering items as they do so.

Scientific Name:	Anas crecca
Identifying Features:	Male has chestnut and blue-green head pattern; female has green speculum
Similar Species:	Garganey
Size:	34–38 cm (13⅜–15 in)
Habitat:	Small ponds and marshes
Population:	Common winter visitor; scarce breeder

Mallard

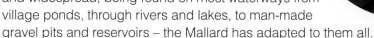

The classic, ubiquitous dabbling duck, from which
most domestic breeds of duck are descended. The
Mallard is often overlooked because it is so common
and widespread, being found on most waterways from
village ponds, through rivers and lakes, to man-made
gravel pits and reservoirs – the Mallard has adapted to them all.
Mallards also have a dark side, noticeable in the breeding season, where gangs of
males will pursue and harass a lone female until she gives in through exhaustion and
mates with them – or occasionally dies trying to fight them off.

The male Mallard is quite simply unmistakeable, with his bottle-green head, yellow bill, white collar and
magenta breast. Mallards are the largest of our dabbling ducks, a useful way to identify females if they
are in a mixed flock with other female dabbling ducks such as Shoveler and Pintail. Females can also be
identified by their prominent speculum: a purplish-blue bordered with white and black at the sides.

Eclipse Plumage

During the summer months, all dabbling ducks undergo a period of moult known as the 'eclipse
plumage', when they are often flightless for a period of time as their new feathers grow. At this time,
male Mallards may resemble a darker version of the female. The key to the Mallard's success is its
adaptability both in its breeding and feeding habits, and its sociable, gregarious nature. Although
most breed in the spring, during mild winters eggs may be laid even before Christmas, with broods of
ducklings out and about by December or January. Mallards are also highly opportunistic and catholic
feeders, taking a wide range of plant and animal food – ducklings are even known to snatch tiny
insects from mid-air.

Scientific Name:	Anas platyrhynchos
Identifying Features:	Male has bottle-green head; female has large size, orange-yellow bill
Similar Species:	Female Gadwall, Shoveler, Pintail
Size:	50–65 cm (19¾–25⅝ in)
Habitat:	Any freshwater
Population:	Abundant

Shoveler

The unique, spoon-shaped bill that gives the Shoveler its popular English name is one of the most extraordinary of all British birds, and allows the Shoveler to feed in its distinctive style. Groups of Shovelers will often feed huddled closely together, driving forward across the surface of the water and hoovering up morsels of food as they go. Oddly, in past times, the name 'shoveler' was also attached to the Spoonbill, and vice versa.

The male Shoveler is the only duck, apart from the much larger and goose-like Shelduck, to show a combination of green, chestnut-brown and white in its plumage, with a bottle-green head, snow-white breast and chestnut flanks. The female also sports the huge, spatula-shaped bill, but otherwise is very similar to other female dabbling ducks, with a speckled brown and buff plumage. In flight the female shows pale greyish-blue on the forewing.

Feeding and Nesting

Like most dabbling ducks, which feed on the surface of the water rather than by diving down beneath it, the Shoveler prefers shallow areas of fresh water, often with reeds or other vegetation where they can take cover should a predator reveal itself.

They usually nest close to water, on the ground amongst low vegetation, without necessarily taking the trouble to conceal themselves, but instead relying on the female's camouflaged plumage. The male is more territorial than other ducks, frequently driving away rivals if they come too close to the nest. When feeding, the broad bill really comes into its own: the Shoveler sucks in water through the sides, where fine hairs act as a filter to trap tiny morsels of animal and plant food.

Scientific Name:	Anas clypeata
Identifying Features:	Huge bill; male has white breast, green head, brown flanks
Similar Species:	Mallard
Size:	44–52 cm (17⅜–20½ in)
Habitat:	Freshwater habitats, especially shallow ones
Population:	Common winter visitor; scarce breeder

Tufted Duck

The commonest and most widespread diving duck in Britain, this smart black and white bird with its distinctive tuft of feathers on the back of the male's head is found in a wide range of freshwater habitats, from huge, concrete-banked reservoirs to park ponds in the heart of our cities. It feeds with a highly effective diving action: using its powerful feet to propel itself down to the bottom of the water to find food.

Like almost all ducks, the male and female Tufted Duck are very different in appearance: so much so that beginners often mistake them for two completely different species. The male is basically black and white: with black head, breast, back and under the tail, and contrasting white flanks.

Identifying Ducks

Look closer and you will see that the 'black' also gives off a purplish sheen, more noticeable in bright sunlight. The eye is bright yellow, and the male also has a prominent black tuft of feathers on his head that gives the species its name. The female, by contrast, is mainly brown, though paler on the flanks in a vague echo of the male's plumage. She too sports a short tuft of feathers, though nothing like as prominent as that of the male. The female may also have a pale patch around her bill, similar to that of the larger and bulkier female Scaup.

Tufted Ducks nest on the ground, often on islands, or in the open but in colonies of gulls or terns which give them protection. The ducklings dive almost as soon as they are hatched, though stay with their parents until they fledge after about seven weeks.

Scientific Name:	Aythya fuligula
Identifying Features:	Male has black and white plumage; female has slight tuft on back of head
Similar Species:	Scaup
Size:	40–47 cm (15¾–18½ in)
Habitat:	Large, open water
Population:	Common, especially in winter

Little Grebe

This tiny grebe (the world's second smallest after the Least Grebe of the Americas) is sometimes mistaken for a baby duck, due to its small size, fluffy plumage and endearing features – hence the widespread folk name still in use, 'dabchick'. It is a widespread and fairly common bird, often overlooked because of its unobtrusive habits.

All year round the Little Grebe can usually be told apart from any other water bird by its diminutive size and fluffy rear end – though beware non-breeding plumage Black-necked Grebes which can also look very small. In spring and summer, Little Grebes adopt a smart breeding dress, with a pale greenish patch at the base of the bill, and a rufous patch on the sides of the face and throat. The rest of the head and body, apart from the paler rear end, is dark brown.

Adaptable Grebes

Little Grebes can be found on some of our smallest waterways, including canals, ponds and marshes – often suitable for no other birds apart from the equally unassuming and ubiquitous Moorhen. They rarely appear on larger areas of water such as reservoirs, though well-vegetated gravel pits are also suitable for breeding and wintering.

Little Grebes are mainly carnivorous, devouring a wide range of aquatic invertebrates, especially insect larvae, molluscs and crustaceans. Like other grebes, they build a floating nest from vegetation, and lay four to six (occasionally as many as 10) eggs. The tiny young are able to swim virtually as soon as they are hatched, but enjoy hitching a ride on the adults' backs for some time afterwards!

Scientific Name:	Tachybaptus ruficollis
Identifying Features:	Small size, fluffy rear end
Similar Species:	Black-necked and Slavonian Grebes
Size:	25–29 cm (9⅞–11½ in)
Habitat:	Freshwater marshes, lakes and ponds
Population:	Common

Great Crested Grebe

The largest European member of its family, the Great Crested Grebe is celebrated for two things: one behavioural, the other historical. It has one of the most elaborate courtship displays of any bird, culminating in the famous 'penguin dance'. The species also played a crucial part in the history of bird protection, being one of the prime reasons for the founding of the Royal Society for the Protection of Birds – formed in the late nineteenth century to prevent the use of grebe skins in women's fashion.

In breeding plumage, both male and female Great Crested Grebes sport an elaborate headdress of orange feathers tipped with brown. In winter, these are discarded, and the bird can best be identified by its large size relative to other grebes, pinkish bill and all-white neck.

Courtship Display

The courtship display often begins very early in the New Year, with male and female facing each other in the water and engaging in a very formal series of head turns and beak twitches. Sometimes this comes to nothing,

but once paired up, they need to cement the bond. This is when they wave weed in each other's faces, while frantically paddling to stay vertically upright in the water – hence the comparison with penguins.

Great Crested Grebes build a floating nest out of water weed, and lay anything between one and six pale, elongated eggs. These are soon stained greenish-brown because of being covered up by water weed to deter predators when the adults are away from the nest. The young are striped like old-fashioned humbugs, and hitch rides on the adults' backs for as long as they are able to.

Scientific Name:	Podiceps cristatus
Identifying Features:	Prominent orange crest (in breeding season only)
Similar Species:	Red-necked Grebe
Size:	46–51 cm (18–20 in)
Habitat:	Gravel pits, rivers and lakes
Population:	Common

Grey Heron

Europe's largest species of heron, the Grey Heron stands up to a metre tall, dwarfing other water birds in the region. In flight, it can resemble a large bird of prey, though its broad, bowed wings, trailing legs and hunched neck make it fairly easy to identify even at a distance or in silhouette. Herons can be unpopular, especially for people who own a garden pond, as they are able to remove exotic fish very effectively.

Grey Herons are tall, elegant birds, most often seen standing by the side of a waterway such as a river, lake or marsh, where they may pose stock-still for several minutes before a rapid movement sees them grab an unwary fish or frog from the water around their feet. They are quite shy, however, and close approach tends to flush them; often uttering a deep, croaky 'fraaank' call as they fly away on sturdy, down-curved wings.

Plumage and Nesting

The plumage is mainly grey, with a paler front (with fine black streaking) and a striking black stripe through the eye, contrasting with the yellow bill. Juveniles lack the black on the head.

Herons are one of the earliest nesting birds, gathering in their colonial heronries soon after the New Year, and adding a few sticks to their huge, untidy nests before settling down to breed. They lay between three and five eggs, which hatch into rather comical-looking youngsters, which remain in the nest being fed by the parents for about seven weeks after hatching. Although rather thin and scraggy in appearance, the heron was considered a delicacy for medieval English kings, though later writers who tried it considered it to have a rather foul taste!

Scientific Name:	Ardea cinerea
Identifying Features:	Large size; grey plumage
Similar Species:	Purple Heron (very rare)
Size:	84–102 cm (33–40 in)
Habitat:	Freshwater marshes, lakes, rivers and ponds
Population:	Common

Coot

Taken for granted by many people because it is so common and ubiquitous, the Coot repays closer attention than it usually gets. During the breeding season, Coots become highly territorial, and will engage in prolonged and vicious fights between individuals, each using their powerful feet to try to force their rival under the water. Outside the breeding season, however, they are gregarious and sociable birds, gathering in flocks numbering in the thousands in some locations.

Seen well, the Coot is hard to confuse with any other species. No other British water bird has the combination of all-black plumage (at closer range actually a very dark grey as well as black) offset by a white bill and face-shield – a feature which gave rise to the saying 'as bald as a Coot'. Juvenile birds are smaller and greyer than the adults, with pale beneath; while downy chicks may be confused with their close relative the Moorhen on account of the fact that they have red on their heads.

Ground-based Birds

Coots are rarely seen in flight, as like all members of the rail family they are clumsy in the air; while on land they reveal their extraordinary feet: not webbed like ducks, but with small lobes on the edge of each toe, rather like grebes. Coots nest early in the spring, laying between six and 10 eggs in a bulky nest made from plant material, often floating on the water (but secured in the base of a tree or by attaching to some other vegetation).

Outside the breeding season they gather in large flocks, often on much more open water such as reservoirs and gravel pits, where they often accompany dabbling duck flocks.

Scientific Name:	Fulica atra
Identifying Features:	Black plumage; white bill
Similar Species:	Moorhen
Size:	36–38 cm (14⅛–15 in)
Habitat:	Freshwater marshes, rivers and lakes
Population:	Abundant

Moorhen

This unassuming and attractive member of the rail family is found on most small areas of water, often managing to thrive where no other waterbird can. As a result of this ability to live in almost any damp habitat it is one of the commonest and most widespread of all wetland species. The name 'moorhen' derives from the old sense of 'moor' meaning marsh or lake (as in the word 'mere') – so simply means 'bird of the lake'.

Moorhens are members of the rail family, but like the world's other species known as 'gallinules' they have adapted to swim on open water rather than creep about in enclosed vegetation. Seen well, the adult is hard to confuse with any other bird: its combination of purple and brown plumage, offset by a jagged pale line along the flanks, pale under the tail and that gaudy red and yellow bill are unmistakable. Youngsters are duller: mainly brown, with a yellowish bill; but they usually also show the pale undertail and the streaks along the sides that distinguish them from their close relative the Coot.

Floating Nests

Like Coots, Moorhens often build a floating nest out of plant material; but as befits a surprisingly adept climber they will also occasionally nest high up in a bush or tree. They lay between five and nine eggs, and after

hatching the young stay with their parents until fledging – any time between six and 10 weeks later.

After breeding, Moorhens tend to stay close to where they nested, and are virtually never seen on large areas of open water like other water birds. Yet they are also able to colonize new habitats, suggesting that they do take to the wing – though at night, to avoid being caught by aerial predators.

Scientific Name:	Gallinula chloropus
Identifying Features:	Red and yellow bill; whiteundertail
Similar Species:	Coot
Size:	32–35 cm (12⅝–13¾ in)
Habitat:	Freshwater marshes, lakes, ponds, rivers
Population:	Abundant

Common Snipe

The Snipe has long been a favourite bird amongst shooters, because its erratic, zig-zagging flight makes it very difficult to hit. The Snipe also appeals to birders for its attractive plumage and distinctive feeding habits: probing that enormously long bill down into the soft mud in order to feel for underground prey such as worms, which it finds by using sensitive hairs at the tip of its bill. It is also one of the few birds to use a non-vocal sound during display: using specially adapted feathers in its tail to produce a distinctive 'drumming'.

Common Snipe often gather in small flocks on areas of open mud, though their subtly camouflaged plumage means that they can easily conceal themselves against the background vegetation. No other common wader has the Snipe's combination of short legs and long, straight bill; and the attractive, subtle tones of the mainly brown and black plumage are also distinctive.

Breeding Habits

During the breeding season, Common Snipe usually seek out damp grassland such as traditionally managed water meadows – which means that in recent years they have suffered a major decline in developed areas of western Europe, where modern farming methods and the draining of many wetlands have left them with nowhere to breed. As a result, breeding Snipe are now mainly found on protected nature reserves. In autumn and winter they will frequent a wide range of well-vegetated wetland habitats, from flooded fields to freshwater marshes, as well as marshy areas near the coast. When flushed from where they are feeding, they will fly away very fast on rapidly beating wings, zig-zagging from side to side to outwit aerial predators such as Merlins.

Scientific Name:	Gallinago gallinago
Identifying Features:	Short legs; long bill
Similar Species:	Jack Snipe, Woodcock
Size:	25–27 cm (9⅞–10⅝ in)
Habitat:	Freshwater marshes and flooded fields
Population:	Common

Common Redshank

The Redshank is by far the commonest and most widespread medium-sized European wader, found in a wide range of habitats from coastal marsh to inland water meadows. It is sometimes known as 'the sentinel of the marsh', a name given as a result of the Redshank's habit of sounding a noisy alarm call when any intruder – human or animal – enters its breeding territory. For this reason, many other wader species, including Oystercatcher, Ringed Plover and Dunlin, nest near pairs of Redshanks.

Easily the most obvious feature of the Redshank – at least at rest – is the orange-red colour of the legs that give the species its name. These are also visible in flight, when another useful field mark, the white rear edge to the wings, is also easy to see. Like its larger relatives, the Spotted Redshank and Greenshank, it also shows a white rump when flying. Otherwise, the Redshank is a relatively nondescript wading bird: with an olive-brown plumage, mottled with darker shades of brown, which appears brighter during the breeding season. The bill is also tinged with orange-red, and is considerably shorter than that of its two cousins.

Breeding Habits

Although Redshanks primarily winter on or near the coast, often in large mixed flocks of other wader species, they usually breed on meadows and other grassland. Like so many species they have suffered from modern farming methods, which have greatly reduced the amount and quality of the food-rich pasture the species needs to raise a family.

When breeding, Redshanks often perch on a gate or fence post in order to survey their territory and watch out for rival birds and predators. As a result, they are usually very easy to see compared to other waders.

Scientific Name:	Tringa totanus
Identifying Features:	Orange-red legs
Similar Species:	Spotted Redshank, Greenshank
Size:	27–29 cm (10⅝–11½ in)
Habitat:	Freshwater and coastal marshes
Population:	Common

Common Sandpiper

Unlike its close relatives, which are predominately northern breeders, the Common Sandpiper has a wide geographical range stretching from northern Scandinavia all the way south to the Mediterranean Sea, and Ireland and Portugal in the west to central Asia and Japan in the east. Most of these birds migrate south to spend the winter in Africa or southern Asia, although some remain in the western, more maritime, parts of their range, where the winters are milder.

The sight of a Common Sandpiper bobbing up and down as it feeds beside a rushing hillside stream is one of the characteristic sights of upland areas in Britain and much of continental Europe. The dumpy shape, short legs and contrasting dark upperparts and white underparts distinguish it from most other waders, apart from the slightly larger and slimmer Green and Wood Sandpipers. Closer to, the short, yellowish bill, greenish legs and long body are noticeable; while in flight the dark rump separates it from its close relatives, and the whirring wing action from most other waders.

River Bird

Despite its wide geographical range, Common Sandpipers tend to choose similar habitats for breeding: preferring fast-flowing rivers and streams, or clear upland lakes. After breeding the species may be found in almost any area of fresh water, including tiny pools and ditches – anywhere it can find tiny insects or invertebrate food which it picks up with that short but effective bill.

As might be expected for such a common bird, the name 'sandpiper' was originally given to this particular species of sandpiper – despite the fact that it is rarely found on beaches as such. A more appropriate name is one used commonly in the nineteenth century, but which has since died out: 'summer snipe'.

Scientific Name:	Actitis hypoleucos
Identifying Features:	Dumpy shape; short bill
Similar Species:	Green Sandpiper, Wood Sandpiper
Size:	19–21 cm (7 ½–8 ¼ in)
Habitat:	Freshwater marshes, streams
Population:	Common

Kingfisher

This jewel-like creature is surely the most stunningly beautiful of any British – perhaps even European   bird. Tinier than most people imagine (barely bigger than a sparrow), the Kingfisher's dazzling blue and orange plumage, combined with its ability to catch fish by diving into the water from a perch, makes it a favourite amongst birders and the wider public alike. Yet its retiring habits mean it is not always easy to see, despite its bright attire.

Simply unmistakeable: electric blue above, and orange below, with a white throat, orange cheeks and a white streak on the side of the neck. Look closer, if you can, and the subtleties of the Kingfisher's plumage become apparent: the blue shades from dark on the wings to pale on the back and rump. Males and females can be told apart from each other by the colour on the lower part of their bill: dark greyish-black in the male, orange in the female.

Freshwater Bird

Kingfishers are classic birds of freshwater streams and rivers, although in hard winter weather they will move to the coast to find food. Harsh winters used to greatly reduce the population, but the trend towards milder winter weather in north-western Europe has enabled them to thrive.

As their name suggests, they feed mainly on small fish which they catch by plunge-diving below the surface of the water. Once they return to their perch, they bash the fish to stun or kill it, then turn it round to swallow it head first; unless the male has decided to present his catch as a token to the female, in which he will hold it by the tail and offer the head to her!

Scientific Name:	Alcedo atthis
Identifying Features:	Electric blue above, orange below
Similar Species:	None
Size:	16-17 cm (6¼–6¾ in)
Habitat:	Rivers and streams
Population:	Common

Sand Martin

The smallest member of the hirundines (swallows and martins) found in Europe, the Sand Martin is one of the earliest migrants to return from its African winter quarters, with some individuals arriving as early as February and March, while the bulk have got back by mid April. They soon get down to excavating their nests in a sandbank; or if the colony has not been flooded in the winter, tidying up the old nests.

Sand Martins are generally brown and white in colour, making them relatively easy to tell apart from all other European swallows and martins apart from the larger and bulkier Crag Martin. Close to, the pale brown upperparts, white throat and underparts, and the narrow brown breast-band are obvious. Sand Martins are also shorter tailed, shorter winged and more compact-looking than House Martins and Swallows, a feature apparent even at a distance.

Adapting to Habitats

In recent years, Sand Martins have learned to take advantage of a habitat provided by us: choosing to nest in sand and gravel quarries rather than along riverbanks. The advantages are obvious: sand banks along rivers often flood in winter (and even sometimes in spring and summer) – destroying the nest burrow. In recent years, enlightened quarry owners have left sandbanks from year to year so the returning birds can make their home there.

After nesting, the young martins will gather along telegraph wires – often in mixed flocks with their relatives. Then, as autumn nears, they head back south – though not as far as Swallows and House Martins. Most British and west European Sand Martins winter in the west African Sahel Zone rather than southern Africa.

Scientific Name:	Riparia riparia
Identifying Features:	Brown above, white below; brown breast-band
Similar Species:	House Martin, Swallow
Size:	12 cm (4¾ in)
Habitat:	Rivers, sand and gravel quarries
Population:	Common

Grey Wagtail

The name of this species is surely one of the least appropriate of all English bird names – although it does have grey in its plumage the most striking feature is the lemon-yellow underparts and elongated shape. A resident species, it often lives near fast-flowing water, nesting in holes and cavities of stone bridges, just inches away from the torrent. Like other wagtails, it has the endearing habit of pumping its tail up and down while walking along.

The Grey Wagtail is often confused with its slightly smaller relative, the Yellow Wagtail. Both have yellow in the plumage, but whereas the Yellow Wagtail has entirely yellow underparts and greenish upperparts, the Grey Wagtail has a slate-grey head and back; and in the breeding season the male has a smart black throat bordered with white.

Range of Habitats

Although the species is often associated with rivers and streams, it can be found in a range of other habitats, especially outside the breeding season, when it occasionally appears in gardens and along grassy verges,

in the company of its commoner relative the Pied Wagtail. In the breeding season, pairs hold territory along a length of river or stream, and are often seen perched on half-submerged rocks or stones along the edge or the centre of the flow, looking for insects. The nest – a cup made of grass and twigs and lined with hair – is built in a hole or cavity along the bank or in a bridge. The female lays four to six eggs, which are incubated for 11-13 days. The young fledge and leave the nest two weeks later, and the adults often have a second, and sometimes even a third, brood.

Scientific Name:	Motacilla cinerea
Identifying Features:	Lemon-yellow underparts; grey back; long tail
Similar Species:	Yellow Wagtail
Size:	17–20 cm (6¾–7⅞ in)
Habitat:	Rivers and streams
Population:	Common

Pied Wagtail

The Pied Wagtail (known elsewhere in Europe and North America as the White Wagtail) is one of the most familiar of all garden birds; yet it is easily overlooked as it goes about its business, feeding on tiny insects picked up from the cracks between paving stones or the surface of the pavement itself. But when Pied Wagtails take to the wing, and utter their distinctive two-syllable call, they are much more likely to be noticed.

One of the most distinctive of all European songbirds, with a combination of black, white and grey that gives the species its name. The race found in Britain, Ireland and parts of continental Europe has a darker back than the 'White' Wagtail, whose pale grey upperparts contrast with the darker head and tail. All races of the species have a white face, dark breast and white belly; and of course the long tail, constantly wagged while the bird is walking.

Urban Roosts

Pied Wagtails are well known for their association with human beings, and are one of the most urban of all our birds, able to thrive in built-up areas. They have taken advantage of this in several ways: most notably in their habit of gathering together in large flocks to roost for the night, especially during the winter months.

These roosts are often in well-lit, man-made areas such as high streets, shopping malls, service stations and car parks – anywhere with a few trees, plenty of light to keep the predators away, and the extra heat generated by buildings to keep the birds warm. Yet despite the noisy contact calls they make to each other as they gather just before dusk, many people are still oblivious to the activity going on just above their heads, before the birds settle down to sleep.

Scientific Name:	Motacilla alba
Identifying Features:	Black and white plumage; long tail
Similar Species:	None
Size:	18 cm (7 in)
Habitat:	Gardens, roadsides
Population:	Abundant

Sedge Warbler

One of the great long-distance migrants of the Old World, Sedge Warblers travel thousands of miles in just two or three hops from their European breeding grounds to their winter quarters in Africa, well south of the Sahara. To do so they feed frantically in the weeks before they depart, putting on a thick layer of fat beneath their skin to enable them to travel so far with only a few 'pitstops' for feeding along the way.

The first sign that Sedge Warblers have returned to their breeding areas in wetlands across northern Europe and Asia is usually the sight of the male launching himself into the air from a low, scrubby bush and singing his song – a collection of excitable notes and phrases sounding like a jazz musician playing an impromptu tune. A close look at the singer reveals a small, streaked bird – basically brown above and paler buff below, with a pale throat and distinctive buffish yellow eye-stripe – the easiest way to distinguish the Sedge Warbler from its close relative the Reed Warbler.

Arctic Breeder

In contrast to other members of its genus, which are mostly confined to middle latitudes with temperate climates, the Sedge Warbler breeds right up into the high Arctic, reaching well into the Arctic Circle. Like other Arctic breeders, it takes advantage of the abundance of insects found in the long summer days; but like them, it must raise a family quickly before the nights start to draw in and the food supply disappears.

In their winter quarters, Sedge Warblers are mainly solitary, and can be found across a broad swathe of Africa from Senegal in the west to Ethiopia in the east, and all the way down to Cape Province in South Africa.

Scientific Name:	Acrocephalus schoenobaenus
Identifying Features:	Streaked plumage
Similar Species:	Reed Warbler
Size:	13 cm (5 in)
Habitat:	Freshwater marshes and reedbeds
Population:	Common

Reed Warbler

One of the best adapted birds to a reedbed existence, the Reed Warbler has an incredible ability to clamber about its habitat of vertical stems in order to find its food – mainly tiny insects, spiders and the odd snail. It also builds its nest in the reeds: suspending a neat cup-shaped structure made from grass, reed stems, leaves and spiders' webs, by weaving it around the stems of the reeds so that it stays in place.

The Reed Warbler is *the* characteristic bird of spring and summer in freshwater reedbeds across Europe and western Asia – its breeding range spanning as far north as Scandinavia and as far south as Morocco, and from Ireland in the west to Iran in the east. Like other members of its genus it is a fairly skulking creature, usually first located by its distinctive song: a series of repeated notes, usually given in twos and threes, with a deep, throaty tone.

Victim of the Cuckoo

When seen (usually on sunny, windless days as it perches on a reed stem), it reveals itself as an unremarkable little bird, brown above (with a slightly warm tinge to the rump), and paler buff below, with a fairly obvious whitish throat, which often stands out when the male is singing.

Reed Warblers are one of the most frequent hosts of the Cuckoo. After the young Cuckoo has hatched, it will use its strength to throw out any remaining Reed Warbler eggs or chicks; after which the unsuspecting host parents will continue to feed it until it fledges. All Reed Warblers are transcontinental migrants, with the entire European and west Asian population migrating south, across the Sahara Desert, to spend the winter in tropical and equatorial Africa.

Scientific Name:	*Acrocephalus scirpaceus*
Identifying Features:	Plain brown, unstreaked plumage
Similar Species:	Marsh Warbler, Sedge Warbler
Size:	13 cm (5 in)
Habitat:	Reedbeds
Population:	Common

Reed Bunting

Unlike most other members of its family, which are mainly birds of farmland or the open steppe grasslands of Asia, the Reed Bunting generally prefers wetland habitats, always nesting where the soil is moist. It has one of the broadest breeding ranges of any bunting, being able to breed anywhere from the high Arctic regions of northern Scandinavia to the very southern-most tip of Europe in Andalucía in southern Spain.

In breeding plumage, the male Reed Bunting is a handsome and very distinctive bird: sporting a jet-black head, face and throat, offset by a snow-white collar and white line from the base of the bill to the neck. In winter he loses his finery, though head and throat remain dark. The female, by contrast, is basically a rather nondescript, streaky chestnut brown, with the best diagnostic feature at all times of the year being the white outer tail feathers, easily seen in flight.

Song

For such a handsome bird, the Reed Bunting's song is rather disappointing: a hesitant series of notes, sounding rather like a bored sound engineer doing a microphone test: 'One... two... testing...'

Reed Buntings, like so many seed-eating birds dependent on farmland for food in autumn and winter, have declined heavily in recent years. This is almost entirely due to modern farming methods, which plant crops all year round and leave little or no 'waste' seed for the birds to feed on in the autumn and winter months. As a result, Reed Buntings have followed the example of several other seed-eating birds, and now turn up regularly in gardens, where they can take advantage of food provided by us.

Scientific Name:	Emberiza schoeniclus
Identifying Features:	Male has black head and white collar; white outer tail feathers
Similar Species:	Corn Bunting, House Sparrow
Size:	15–16 cm (5⁷⁄₈–6¹⁄₄ in)
Habitat:	Reedbeds (summer); farmland, marshes (winter)
Population:	Common

Coastal

Species

Coastal Species

Where the sea meets the land, birders often meet birds. It is a rich convergence, making up such distinctive habitats as estuaries, sand-dunes, beaches, sea-cliff, offshore islands and river inlets, each with their own favoured birds. And this is apart from the sea itself, which contains plenty of food for birds. Coastlines are also excellent places to watch migration, since following the sea allows an uncluttered journey, and the edge of land is there for safety from storms.

Many of our most familiar birds are primarily coastal. These include the many sea birds, such as terns, gulls, cormorants, auks, gannets and shearwaters, plus those that are essentially water birds, such as ducks. Waders use the juxtaposition of land and sea to feed on the inter-tidal multitudes found in mud or sand, mainly worms, molluscs and crustaceans – and indeed, there are few coastal birds that do not eat animals from these groups.

On the whole, coastal birds tend to differ from other birds by being essentially large bodied. There are only a small number of passerines in this biome. Furthermore, most coastal birds are dark above and pale below, remaining cryptic to predators looking down and to food items, such as fish, looking up.

Many of our coastal birds change their spots in the breeding season, and become birds of the tundra. Sea Ducks are typical in this regard, and they swap the worm-mollusc-crustacean diet for the abundant insects on and around freshwater tundra bogs and pools. For some, this is a major dietary change.

Another feature of coastal birds is that, on the whole, they are great travellers. Like the shifting seas themselves, they seem perpetually on the move; some, indeed, such as the Arctic Tern, routinely span the globe.

Shelduck

With its long neck, ease of gait, comparatively large size and similarity of plumage between male and female – none of which are typical duck features – the Shelduck seems to fit midway between a duck and a goose, and is not closely related to the rest of the ducks. It is, however, usually found in company with them, either feeding over the mud of an estuary or salt marsh, or swimming alongside them at gravel pits and other freshwater sites inland.

This conspicuous species has a number of interesting behavioural quirks. The most frequent nest-site, for example, is an old rabbit hole, although birds will also use other natural holes and occasional artificial ones. Such sites may be eight metres (26 ft) off the ground, giving the young birds an interesting start to life when they have to jump out. Once hatched, they are led to a nursery area, where they join the other local broods and learn to feed for themselves.

Aunties

Curiously, though, before the young are fully grown, the adults depart the area and leave their young in the care of a few non-breeding adults, known as 'aunties', who oversee their development to adulthood. The parents, meanwhile, take a short easterly flight to a huge area of mudflats on the north coast of Germany, part of the region known as the Waddensee. Here they gather with other adults from all over Europe and moult, losing their wing feathers almost simultaneously and becoming flightless for a period. Only when the moult is fully complete do they return to their wintering or breeding areas.

The salt marshes in Britain and in Germany provide Shelducks with a diet of inter-tidal invertebrates, including worms, shrimps and – a great favourite – a small snail known as Hydrobia.

Scientific Name:	Tadorna tadorna
Identifying Features:	Bottle-green head and neck; chestnut breast-band
Similar Species:	Goosander, Avocet
Size:	58–67 cm (22⅞–26⅜ in)
Habitat:	Estuaries, salt marshes, dunes, gravel pits
Population:	Common

Fulmar

At first sight the Fulmar resembles a gull, being of similar size and having basically grey and white plumage. The flight style soon gives it away, though; instead of the gulls' languid motion, the Fulmar flies on wings held rigidly out, alternating bouts of quick flaps with long, stiff-winged glides. Those long, narrow wings enable the Fulmar to fly for enormous distances, riding the sea currents with supreme efficiency. It is thus very much a sea bird, often seen out in the very depths of the ocean, hundreds of kilometres from land.

Out on the ocean the Fulmar eats a variety of sea animals, including squid (a favourite), fish, crustaceans and marine worms, all of them seized by a quick lunge when the bird is swimming, or occasionally during a brief dive. The Fulmar's bill is strong, with a hooked tip, allowing it to pick off pieces of meat from the floating carcasses of sea mammals, another useful food source on the open ocean. Fulmars will also compete in the scrum of sea birds feeding on offal thrown out from trawlers.

Eggs and Chicks

Fulmars breed on sea cliffs and islands, usually on a ledge but sometimes on an earthy slope. They lay a single egg not in a nest, but more or less directly upon the substrate (whether it be rocky, earthy or other), although a few artistic pairs add a stone for lining. The egg is then incubated for an extraordinarily long time, sometimes up to 53 days; the female starts and then has a week off to recuperate from egg laying. Not surprisingly, having invested so much effort, the parents are very protective of their hatched chick, never leaving it for the first two weeks. Fulmars are also capable of spitting an extremely foul-smelling concoction of stomach-oil at any intruders, a talent that the young inherit in the nest. Remarkably, if the young Fulmar survives its nestling phase and reaches fledging at 46 days, it has a long haul to adulthood: some individuals do not breed until they are 12 years old. They may reach an age of 50 or more.

Scientific Name:	Fulmarus glacialis
Identifying Features:	Long, parallel-edged wings; thick bill
Similar Species:	Gulls, Manx Shearwater
Size:	45–50 cm (17³⁄₄–19³⁄₄ in)
Habitat:	Breeds on sea cliffs; winters at sea
Population:	Common

Gannet

The Gannet is one of the largest sea birds in the world and, with its long, black-tipped white wings, long bill and pointed tail, it is also one of the most distinctive. It flies over the sea with slow, languid wing beats alternated with long glides, and it breaks this relaxed pattern only when it spots some food below. It then gains height to 30 m (100 ft) or more above the surface, checks below and then tumbles into a spectacular nosedive, closing its wings at the last moment and making a splash on impact.

The Gannet finds and catches its food, medium-sized fish. It specializes in shoaling species such as herring and cod, and the sight of one Gannet feeding often brings others in. In order to cope with their extreme feeding method, Gannets have forward-facing eyes to judge their dives, air-sacs under the skin to absorb the shock of plunges, and nostrils opening internally to the bill to prevent water being forced up them.

Cliff-top Colonies

Gannets breed in large colonies on northern sea-cliffs and rocky islands, often tightly packed together. Pairs mate for life and have a series of entertaining displays to keep the bond strong, including a mutual 'fencing' of the bills combined with bowing. The male builds a nest out of seaweed, feathers, grass and earth cemented together by the birds' droppings, making a pile at least 30 cm (12 in) high, but reaching as high as 2 m (6.5 ft) over the years. Just a single egg is laid each year, and it hatches, if all goes well, after 42–46 days. The young Gannet is fed by both parents on regurgitated fish. The adults may make very long round-trips, of 400 km (250 miles) or more, just to find food for a single visit. After some 80 days the adults cease their endeavour and no longer visit; after a week or so, the youngster gets the message and leaves to begin the long road – five to six years – to breeding maturity.

Scientific Name:	Sula bassana
Identifying Features:	Dagger-shaped bill; orange-yellow on adult head
Similar Species:	None
Size:	87–100 cm (34¼–39⅜ in)
Habitat:	Breeds on rocky cliffs or islands; winters at sea
Population:	Numerous breeding bird, common offshore

Cormorant

For a water bird, it is surprising how little time the Cormorant actually spends in the water. If it has a ready supply of food, this large fish-eater may only spend a few minutes each day actually foraging, while the rest of the time it simply sits out on a perch such as a rock, a jetty or the branch of a tree, and watches the world go by. As it does so, it often holds out its wings in characteristic fashion, allowing them to dry.

Indeed, for a water bird, the Cormorant is not very waterproof. The drying of the wings is necessary because the body feathers, apart from an inner layer of down, are specially adapted to absorb, not repel water, so that the Cormorant is not too buoyant. When feeding, it chases fish underwater using its back-set feet to propel it, so it pays to be able to sink easily. The Cormorant's bones are denser than most other birds', reducing buoyancy, and the Cormorant will also swallow stones to help it dive. The Cormorant's eyes are also special; they can adapt to seeing equally well in water and air.

Food Supply

Most of the fish that the Cormorant catches are bottom-dwellers, especially flatfish, but the Cormorant is quite adaptable. Most live on cliffs and do their fishing in the sea, but small and increasing numbers breed inland, nesting in trees and feeding on the fish of rivers or lakes.

The seasonal 'badge' to attract a mate is when the male opens its wings and flashes its white thigh patch. Both sexes contribute to building a large platform of sticks and debris, upon which the three to four eggs are laid. Cormorants usually nest in colonies, and theft of nest material is commonplace. After 30 days the eggs hatch and the young – brown with white bellies – then enjoy up to three months of being fed.

Scientific Name:	Phalacrocorax carbo
Identifying Features:	Long neck; heavy bill; white on thighs in breeding season
Similar Species:	Shag
Size:	80–100 (31½–39⅜ in)
Habitat:	Sea coasts; inland lakes and rivers
Population:	Common

Oystercatcher

With its distinctive black and white plumage, plump shape and that amazing orange bill, it is hard to mistake the Oystercatcher for any other bird. Although primarily a coastal species, Oystercatchers are adaptable creatures, and have been known to nest and feed in a wide range of habitats, including grassland, golf courses, gravel pits and even the roofs of industrial estates. But they remain a quintessential bird of the coast, gathering in huge flocks to exploit the food-rich mud revealed at every low tide.

A characteristic trilling, piping call is often the first indication of the presence of Oystercatchers on a coastal marsh or beach; soon followed by the sight of these plump, sociable birds cruising low in flight, or stopping to feed along the exposed mud on the tideline. No other wader has the Oystercatcher's distinctive plumage: black above and on the upper chest; pure white below; with short, stumpy pink legs. But the most obvious feature is the thick, straight, orange bill – likened by some observers to a carrot – which the Oystercatcher uses to probe deep into soft sand or mud in order to reach its favourite food; not oysters, but cockles, mussels and other shellfish.

Shellfish Wars

Their ability to eat cockles has brought them into conflict with shellfish gatherers, although in fact the Oystercatcher is an adaptable feeder, and will often gather in freshly ploughed fields to pick up earthworms.

The courtship display of the Oystercatcher is an elaborate one: birds will dip their bill downwards and approach their mate, piping as they go. Once paired up, the birds nest in a scrape on the ground, making them very vulnerable to mammal predators.

Scientific Name:	Haematopus ostralegus
Identifying Features:	Pied plumage; huge orange bill
Similar Species:	None
Size:	40–45 cm (15¾–17¾ in)
Habitat:	Coastal marshes and beaches
Population:	Common

Ringed Plover

The Ringed Plover is an unassuming little wader with a fascinating story to tell regarding its migration. Whereas birds nesting in temperate latitudes, such as the British Isles, move fairly short distances south for the winter, those nesting in the High Arctic regions undertake major migratory journeys, heading thousands of kilometres south to Africa. This strategy, known as 'leapfrog migration', is thought to have evolved as the species expanded its breeding range to the north after the last Ice Age.

The Ringed Plover is a typical bird of shorelines, coastal marshes and beaches throughout coastal Britain and Europe, and is also sometimes found inland, where it may feed and breed in the same locations as its smaller relative the Little Ringed Plover.

Identifying Plovers

With close attention it is fairly straightforward to tell the two species apart: the Ringed Plover is larger and bulkier, and much less elegant on the wing. Its orange legs, orange base to the bill and pale wing-bar are all key identification features, and also help distinguish it from its other close European relative, the Kentish

Plover. When breeding, Ringed Plovers generally nest on the bare ground or amongst low vegetation, where their blotchy eggs can be well camouflaged. If approached, the adult will often move away from the nest or chicks and begin a 'distraction display'. This involves stretching out its wing as if it is broken, as a trick to lure away predators such as foxes.

Unlike many other waders, Ringed Plovers are rarely seen in large flocks during the autumn and winter, but will often gather in small groups with other species, picking small items off the surface of the mud.

Scientific Name:	Charadrius hiaticula
Identifying Features:	Orange base to bill; orange legs; wing-bar in flight
Similar Species:	Little Ringed Plover
Size:	18–20 cm (7–7⁷⁄₈ in)
Habitat:	Coastal marshes, beaches
Population:	Common

Turnstone

With its short bill and legs, dumpy shape and characteristic tortoiseshell plumage pattern, the Turnstone is one of the easiest to identify of all waders. It is also equally easy to appreciate how it operates, and how it gets its name. The feeding method is based on using its bill to turn over objects, including stones but also seaweed, shells and all manner of tideline debris to see what edible items might be hidden underneath. It is capable of shifting objects weighing up to about 100 g (3.5 oz) and, if something is too large and bulky, it will sometimes gather a small team to heave it away together.

These birds have a distinctly catholic diet, wider than that of any other wader. Apart from the expected molluscs (mussels, periwinkles), crustaceans (crabs, barnacles) and worms, it also eats fish, sea urchins and a variety of edible scraps thrown out by people. It will scavenge on dead animals (even a human corpse has been recorded) and take eggs from the nests of sea birds. It has also been seen feasting on a bar of soap. Meanwhile, on the tundra where it nests, its main sustenance actually comes from insects.

Flock Hierarchy

Turnstones are sociable creatures, living in small groups, but they are not necessarily friendly. Flocks have strict hierarchies, and the dominant birds in each group tend to hog the best feeding opportunities. The hierarchy is maintained easily, because each bird has an individually recognizable face pattern. If a bird attempts to feed outside its allotted station, it might be attacked or even killed.

In the breeding season Turnstones are found in the tundra zone of the High Arctic, where they prefer sites near water, usually close to the coast. The nest may be in the open or concealed, and contains the usual wader complement of four eggs. As so often happens among this family of birds when they nest this far north, the young tend only to be overseen in their later stages by one parent, in this case the male.

Scientific Name:	*Arenaria interpres*
Identifying Features:	White belly; thick bill; tortoiseshell pattern on back when breeding
Similar Species:	Purple Sandpiper
Size:	22–24 cm (8⅝–9½ in)
Habitat:	Rocky coastlines
Population:	Common winter visitor

Dunlin

The Dunlin is the ubiquitous small wader across much of the coastal areas of the Northern Hemisphere, being equally common and widespread on both sides of the Atlantic Ocean, and also found in Asia. Nesting in a wide range of locations and habitats, Dunlins do not travel so far outside the breeding season as many other waders, with virtually all wintering in the Northern Hemisphre, and only a handful ever making it beyond the Equator.

In breeding plumage, the Dunlin is a striking and distinctive little bird, with a chestnut-brown back contrasting with a black belly. The bill is also an obvious feature: decurved, and varying considerably in length, depending which particular race the individual bird belongs to. Outside the breeding season, after moulting into its winter plumage, the Dunlin's name – meaning 'brown-coloured bird' – is more appropriate. Having lost the rich chestnut and black, wintering Dunlins are a grey-brown colour, with paler underparts. At this time of year they can be confused with a variety of other small to medium-sized waders including the larger Knot and much paler Sanderling.

An Adaptable Bird

Much of the Dunlin's success comes down to its adaptability: it is equally at home on beaches, coastal and freshwater marshes and even riverbanks – and on migration may be seen almost anywhere with a patch of wet mud where the birds can stop to refuel.

When breeding, Dunlins seek out a wide range of grassy areas, from coastal meadows to upland moors, where its distinctive trilling call is a characteristic part of the scene. As ground-nesters they are especially vulnerable to mammal predators, and as a result many pairs must make several breeding attempts before they are successful.

Scientific Name:	Calidris alpina
Identifying Features:	Down-curved bill; black belly in summer
Similar Species:	Knot, Sanderling
Size:	16–20 cm (6¼–7⅞ in)
Habitat:	Coasts, marshes
Population:	Abundant

Curlew

The Curlew is the largest European wader, and one of the best-known, being found in a wide range of habitats from coastal marshes and beaches to high moorland, where its far-carrying call is a characteristic spring and summer sound. The call – rather than the curved bill – is also the origin of the species' name, although the species has a large and varied vocal repertoire, including a haunting, bubbling call often delivered in flight.

Seen well, the Curlew cannot be confused with any other wader, being appreciably larger than both the godwits and Whimbrel, and with a much longer, strongly decurved bill – up to one quarter of its entire body length. The plumage is generally buffish brown in tone, with delicate and intricate markings visible at close range, streaked underparts and a plain, pale area under the tail. The legs are very long and greenish in colour.

Nesting

In the southern parts of its European breeding range, the Curlew is generally a bird of upland areas, nesting at between 500 and 700 m (1,650 and 2,300 ft) above sea level on moorland, peat bogs and heaths. Like most nesting waders it dislikes heavily vegetated or forested landscapes, preferring to nest where it can easily see for a wide range around it, so it can take evasive action should a predator approach the nest.

After breeding, Curlews usually head to the coast. Like other maritime waders, it follows a tidal regime: feeding when low tide exposes extensive areas of open mud, where it can probe that huge bill deep down in search of invertebrate prey. As the waters rise, it makes a twice-daily journey to an area of higher ground where it is able to rest amongst waders for safety and security until the tide retreats again.

Scientific Name:	Numenius arquata
Identifying Features:	Large size; very long, decurved bill
Similar Species:	Whimbrel
Size:	50–60 cm (19¾–23⅝ in)
Habitat:	Coastal marshes and beaches; moorland when breeding
Population:	Common

Black-headed Gull

'Sea gull' is never a very accurate term, and no species shoots down the concept quite like the Black-headed Gull. In the winter this elegant species, with its slender wings with sharp points, its red legs and its smudge behind the eye, is found all over inland Britain, in huge flocks on reservoirs, in wheeling groups at rubbish tips, following the plough and competing with ducks for slices of thrown-out bread.

Bizarrely, the Black-headed Gull does not have a black head at any stage of its life; in the breeding season it merely has a very smart chocolate-brown hood, with a neat white eye-ring. The colour is at least dark, and the hood plays an important part in communication, as well as probably absorbing the sun's light to prevent glare to the eye. When being aggressive, Black-headed Gulls usually bow their heads towards a rival, whether on land or water.

Omnivorous Eater

In common with most gulls, the Black-headed Gull is impressively omnivorous. Its main food in winter is invertebrates found in the soil, especially worms, while its main diet on the breeding grounds, where these are coastal, is marine invertebrates. However, these gulls also eat all kinds of scraps, grain, berries and insects, and will fly around swarming ants on hot summer days.

The species breeds in often large and invariably extremely noisy colonies; the calls are harsher and less trumpeting in tone than those of larger species. Pairs defend a small territory on a patch of shingle, marsh, dune or moorland. The female lays two to three eggs in a neat pile of vegetation, and incubates them for 23–26 days. Youngsters need to avoid trespassing on to their neighbours' territory, for they could elicit a violent response.

Scientific Name:	Larus ridibundus
Identifying Features:	Red legs and bill; white isosceles triangle at front of outer wing
Similar Species:	Common Gull, Mediterranean Gull, Kittiwake

Size:	34–37 cm (13⅜–14⅝ in)
Habitat:	Breeds in salt marshes; inland within reach of freshwater
Population:	Common breeding bird; abundant in winter

Common Gull

One look at the Common Gull and you might easily guess that it was not as predatory as most of its fellow gulls. It has a much thinner bill than a Herring Gull, for example, and, for what it is worth, its face carries a much gentler expression. The facts bear out this impression. The Common Gull does not normally feed on young birds or small mammals, instead confining itself to smaller creatures such as worms, insects and other invertebrates.

It is, however, still a successful and resourceful bird. It does, for example, occur both on the coast and inland, breeding and wintering on both. It also utilizes all kinds of food sources from rubbish dumps (although less habitually than many gulls) to berries, and from fish to carrion. Intriguingly, it is also remarkably adaptable in where it places its nest. Some nests are on the ground in conventional gull fashion, in dunes, rocks and beaches, whereas others are in more unusual sites, including on mats of floating vegetation, gravel roofs of buildings and trees, especially tree stumps. In such eclectic places the Common Gull builds differently; on the ground the nest is little more than a lined scrape, while tree and marsh nests are quite substantial heaps of vegetation.

Solitary Tendencies

Common Gulls are sometimes colonial, but they have more of a tendency than some gulls to nest alone. They lay the usual gull tally of three eggs which are incubated for 23–28 days. Chicks on the ground may leave the nest early, while those in elevated sites stay put.

The Common Gull is noted for its voice, even among such a clamorous group of birds. Its calls are often higher pitched than the rest, and, with imagination, the American name of Mew Gull seems vaguely appropriate. But really, it would be a cat in distress, such is the ear-splitting nature of some of its squeals.

Scientific Name:	Larus canus
Identifying Features:	Black on wing-tip with large white blob; grey on back
Similar Species:	Herring Gull, Kittiwake
Size:	40–42 cm (15¾–16½ in)
Habitat:	Marshes, lakes when breeding; inland freshwater in winter
Population:	Common

Lesser Black-backed Gull

Among the region's club of very similar-looking gulls, it is very easy for this species to get lost in the crowd. Often mistaken for the brutish Great Black-backed Gull, this is a far more elegant and graceful species, with different breeding habitats and a much stronger mastery of the air. The Lesser Black-back is closely related to the Herring Gull but, once again, it is subtly different: more liable to be seen out to sea, far more migratory and, once again, a far more efficient flying machine.

Much has changed in the life of the Lesser Black-backed Gull in the last 30 or 40 years. British birds, and some of their Continental counterparts, used to be migrants, travelling to the Mediterranean region, or even further, for the winter. Now, with conditions suiting them further north (perhaps more food available, perhaps climatic amelioration), they tend to stay put and winter 'at home'. Young birds might still make the journey, but the adults tend not to. In the meantime, the Scandinavian versions of the Lesser Black-backed Gull also flood Britain in the winter. These gulls have much darker backs than their British breeding counterparts, making them look like Great Black-backed Gulls – no wonder people get confused.

Gull Colonies

The Lesser Black-backed Gull breeds in typically gull-infested sites in summer, such as sand dunes and shingle banks; it also frequently nests inland, on moorland. It usually forms colonies and these can be very large, and they are often mixed colonies with Herring Gulls. The two keep apart because of, among other things, their subtly different displays; when proclaiming territory, for example, Lesser Black-backs lift their heads higher than Herring Gulls. The Lessers also breed in areas with more vegetation cover, and their nests are more densely packed in. In common with other gulls, the Lesser Black-back lays an average of three eggs, which hatch after 24–27 days. After another month the young fly, and it will then be at least three years before they begin to breed themselves.

Scientific Name:	Larus fuscus
Identifying Features:	White spots on wing-tips; dark back; long wings
Similar Species:	Great Black-backed Gull, Herring Gull, Yellow-legged Gull
Size:	52–67 cm (20½–26⅜ in)
Habitat:	Breeds on coastal dunes and islands
Population:	Common

Herring Gull

The irrepressible Herring Gull is an abundant, successful and somewhat boorish bird – the sort that it is very difficult to overlook. It is most overbearing on the coast, where its many wailing calls make up an important part of the seaside atmosphere. Although primarily a breeding bird of cliffs, dunes or beaches, it thinks nothing of living out its nesting season, with its noisy triumphs and disasters, on the flat roofs of coastal towns, commuting no great distance to rubbish dumps, dockyards and the nearest beach.

Herring Gulls are usually very sociable, and most of the population breeds in colonies. Pair formation actually usually occurs away from the breeding centres, at gathering spots known as 'clubs', while the colonies themselves are usually subdivided into neighbourhoods where egg-laying and hatching is closely synchronized. Gull society is full of complicated gestures, including head-nodding, facing away or standing erect, all combining into a universally understood sign language that oils the wheels of social cohesion. Between males and females the most important gestures are actually very practical; for much of the period before and during egg-laying, the male brings in offerings of food for the female, to save her the trouble of feeding herself. Many times a day, the provider male arrives on the territory and throws up chivalrously, often goaded by open-mouthed begging postures from the female.

Herring Gull Society

There are several interesting quirks that happen in Herring Gull society. Sometimes females form pairs with other females and, aided by sperm from 'donor' males, may actually raise chicks. And the chicks themselves, of which there are usually three to a brood, will sometimes abandon their parents and attempt to be adopted by their neighbours, whom they deem to be better suppliers of food. Usually, however, the young gulls remain with their parents for the 35–40 days they take to gain full flight.

Scientific Name:	Larus argentatus
Identifying Features:	Pale eye and low crown; white blobs on wing-tips
Similar Species:	Yellow-legged Gull, Lesser Black-backed Gull, Common Gull, Glaucous Gull
Size:	55–67 cm (21¾–26⅜ in)
Habitat:	Coasts; inland waters and dumps
Population:	Abundant

Great Black-backed Gull

The world's largest gull, the Great Black-backed Gull does not hesitate to throw its weight about. It commonly steals food from other bird species, including other gulls; it is at the top of every gull hierarchy; and it is also one of the most predatory species, having no hesitation in eating young sea birds and sometimes adults, too. It has a thick, powerful neck and body, a truly fearsome bill with sharp cutting edges, and a mean-looking small eye amidst a frowning expression.

This is one of the more marine gulls, generally uncommon away from the coast. It will be found on inland rubbish dumps and some large wetlands, but it has not expanded to the land like many other species. Nevertheless, it is just as omnivorous and opportunistic as the other species. It is a frequent visitor to fishing boats when the catch is made, it will regularly resort to eating carrion, and on the beach it will often drop shellfish down on to a hard surface while flying, in order to break them open. It even has the dexterity, on occasion, to catch birds in flight.

Colonies and Calls

For breeding, Great Black-backed Gulls are usually found on sea cliffs and rocky islands. Flatter sites such as marshes, beaches and even flat rooftops are far less frequently used. It can be colonial, but has a tendency to breed alone that is rather more pronounced than for other gulls. Appropriately, perhaps, it often selects the topmost part of a cliff, or some other eminence, as if to lord it over the other birds nearby. Breeding birds are quite vocal, giving a marvellously gruff and bad-tempered range of calls.

Great Black-backs build a typical gull mound of grass, seaweed and other plant material for the nest, and lay the regulation two to three eggs. Both adults incubate, and look after their chicks with a tenderness quite out of keeping with the general character of this bird.

Scientific Name:	Larus marinus
Identifying Features:	Pitch-black back with large white spots on tips; broad, blunt wings
Similar Species:	Lesser Black-backed Gull
Size:	64–78 cm (25⅛–30¾ in)
Habitat:	Mainly coastal; some inland dumps or lakes
Population:	Common

Kittiwake

The Kittiwake is the acceptable face of the gull family. It lives a blameless life of eating fish and crustaceans and spends no time harassing other gulls or victimizing young sea birds in that overweening way that other species have. It has a mild, gentle expression to go with its demeanour. And it never shows up in the insalubrious surroundings of the rubbish dump. Indeed, it is really a proper sea bird, keeping a healthy lifestyle in the marine air.

The odd name comes from the Kittiwake's call. Birds at the breeding colony are exceptionally boisterous (it is a true gull, after all), uttering the bird's name incessantly in a sort of pleading, complaining, and often ear-splitting manner. The sound often rebounds off the precipitous cliffs where this species breeds, the noise mixing with the waves and creating an atmosphere of wildness and urgency.

Cliff-top Homes

The nests are remarkable. They are platforms made from mud collected from nearby freshwater pools, seaweed and grass, and they are distinctly better built structures than those of other gulls. They need to be, too. Most are placed on the tallest and most precipitous of sea-cliffs, often lodged on to small rock projections, and they can look highly precarious with the frightening drop below them. However, they are very safe from predators. There are usually two eggs instead of the usual three for a gull, and the youngsters, when they are hatched, stay still on the platform instead of wandering around and risking an early death.

Once the young have left the nest, Kittiwakes leave the coast and venture out to sea, often hundreds of miles offshore. Here they find food by dipping down to the surface in flight, or even making short plunges to a metre or so down. They often accompany whales and other sea mammals on their travels around the oceans of the Northern Hemisphere.

Scientific Name:	Rissa tridactyla
Identifying Features:	Black legs; inky-black wing-tips without white blobs
Similar Species:	Common Gull, Black-headed Gull
Size:	38–40 cm (15–15¾ in)
Habitat:	Sea and cliffs
Population:	Common

Common Tern

Very much the typical tern, the Common Tern has the usual greyish plumage, smart black cap and long, dagger-shaped bill shared by most of the family. It has a long, strongly forked tail and supremely angular wings, with the sharp tips that distinguish them so well from gulls. It flies with very full wing-beats, the wings slightly angled back. Typically, it flies to and fro over shallow water, either fresh or salty, intermittently hovering and plunge-diving down.

Fish are supremely important in the Common Tern's life. They constitute the main diet, and it is only when these are in short supply that this tern will take serious quantities of invertebrates, such as crustaceans. Fish also play an important role in courtship. For much of the immediate period before egg-laying, the male brings fish to the female every day to help her get into peak condition; this provision is of great importance to the pair bond. If the provider slips below the expected six-per-hour provisioning rate, the partnership could split up. The condition of the eggs could also be compromised: the more efficiently the female is fed, the larger the eggs she will lay and the healthier the young will be.

Nesting

Common Terns will nest as an isolated pair, but far more often they gather into colonies, which are usually quite substantial, with 200 or more nests. The usual site is on an island or beach and, although this is primarily a coastal species, it frequently nests inland as well, on freshwater lakes and marshes. In typical tern style, the nest would not win any construction prizes, being just a scrape in the ground lined with a few bits of debris. The clutch varies between one and three eggs.

After breeding, Common Terns retreat south to winter in tropical seas. They do not migrate in any rush, and can still be seen into October, or even later.

Scientific Name:	Sterna hirundo
Identifying Features:	Black-tipped red bill; clean black cap; white face and underparts
Similar Species:	Arctic Tern, Roseate Tern, Sandwich Tern
Size:	31–35 cm (12¼–13¾ in)
Habitat:	Breeds on islands and beaches; at sea in winter
Population:	Common

Arctic Tern

Terns are identified on the finest points, and to those who have the experience and confidence, the best way to tell an Arctic Tern is in its manner of flight. Compared to its closely related species, the Arctic has a more bouncy, flickering flight, with a snappier, faster upstroke, and the narrow wings look slightly forward set, rather than centred. When hunting over the sea, this bird has a distinct tendency to hover, descend and then hover again before finally plunging in.

There must be something special in those wings, because the Arctic Tern is famous for having what is perhaps the longest regular migration of any bird in the world – although some shearwaters push it close. Often breeding well into the High Arctic, it travels to the Antarctic, no less, for the winter, swapping one side of the world for the other. It will migrate along coast and sea, but there is evidence to suggest that some birds might take an overland route at great altitude. Once arriving in the Antarctic, some individuals actually fly around that continent and might travel as much as 50,000 km (31,000 miles) in a year altogether. In doing so, they see more daylight in a year than any other living organism.

Nesting and Parenting

On the breeding grounds there are no such wonders; it follows the basic pattern of most of its family. It settles in the tundra, on coasts or even rough pastureland, as long as the vegetation is not too high – it has very short legs. Breeding in colonies, each pair builds a shallow scrape for the one to three eggs, which the parents incubate for three weeks. Up in the north, the diet tends not always to consist of fish, since there is such an abundance of flying insects that the terns take advantage of these.

Once breeding, the Arctic becomes a coastal bird again. Chicks fly at three or four weeks, the beginning of a record-breaking career aloft. One Arctic Tern was known to have lived 29 years – and seen the world over.

Scientific Name:	Sterna paradisaea
Identifying Features:	Longer tail-streamers, narrower wings and shorter legs than Common Tern
Similar Species:	Common Tern, Roseate Tern, Sandwich Tern
Size:	33–35 cm (13–13¾ in)
Habitat:	Coasts, islands, rivers
Population:	Common summer visitor

Guillemot

At first sight the Guillemot looks like a Northern Hemisphere version of a penguin, with its upright stance, small wings and sharply contrasting plumage, dark above and white below. In the water the resemblance remains, as it powers itself below the surface by a rowing action of the wings and with its back-positioned feet. It is only when it takes off on slightly over-fast wing beats, and makes its safely into the air that you realize that it is actually quite a different bird.

In common with the other auks, chasing food underwater is the main method of finding sustenance. In the Guillemot's case this is mainly fish, and it has been known to go down 30 m (100 ft) below the surface and fly out more than 50 km (31 miles) from the colony to get a good supply.

Independent Young

The breeding of Guillemots is in many ways remarkable. They tend to nest on tall cliffs, often occupying very narrow ledges at terrifying heights (up to 300 m/1,000 ft) above the sea. It may be safe, but it is also desperately cramped, because Guillemots have the most densely packed colonies of birds in the world – 20 nests may be crammed into a square metre. They lay a single egg, which is incubated for up to 38 days, although usually less. The egg is intricately marked with squiggles and splodges, and it seems that each is different; their unique eggs help Guillemots find their nest-sites in the crowded colony.

Both sexes incubate and feed the chick until, when only 15–25 days old and only half grown at best, it leaves the nest. Astonishingly, there is only one way to do this – to jump. The young are light, with partly grown wings and, so long as they do not hit rocks or get snatched by predators, they land on the sea safely. Once there, they find their male parent and the two swim out to sea until, after a month, the youngster becomes independent.

Scientific Name:	Uria aalge
Identifying Features:	Dark above and white below; dagger-like bill; black legs
Similar Species:	Razorbill, Puffin, Little Auk
Size:	38–41 cm (15–16⅛ in)
Habitat:	Inshore coasts, cliffs and islands; at sea in winter
Population:	Common

Razorbill

At first sight this auk looks similar to a Guillemot, and indeed its lifestyle, nesting on cliffs but living mainly at sea, is not very different. However, to look at, the Razorbill has a longer tail than the Guillemot, which can be obvious on the water, and its bill is much thicker in profile. As the name suggests, if viewed from above or below, the bill is narrow and file-like, and there is also a smart white stripe near its tip.

In common with the Guillemot, the Razorbill feeds under the water, chasing fish. However, it has a more catholic diet than the Guillemot, frequently incorporating significant numbers of crustaceans, too. It seems unable to dive as deep as a Guillemot, rarely venturing more than 7 m (23 ft) down. Another significant difference between the two species is that, when a Razorbill brings food to its young in the nest, it does not take in just one held lengthwise in the bill, as a Guillemot does, but can carry up to 20, fitted crosswise in the same way as a Puffin.

Razorbills frequently share the same cliffs as Guillemots in the breeding season, but they occupy distinctly different sites, with a little more luxury and a lot more space. Their ledges tend to be wide, often with an overhang, and they will sometimes choose flat sites among rocks and boulders. Just a single egg is laid and incubated by both parents for 36 days.

Leaving the nest carries the same dramas that afflict the young Guillemot. At 18 days old the chick departs the breeding ledge, well before it is fully grown, and does so by a straight jump down to the sea, feeble, undeveloped wings fluttering. In contrast to the Guillemot chicks, however, which leave in the evening during the light, Razorbill chicks wait until 9 p.m. at least, when night has fallen in late summer. This literal leap in the dark is probably good to avoid predators, but the chick's heart must be in its mouth as it casts off into the blackness.

Scientific Name:	Alca torda
Identifying Features:	Broad, thin bill with subterminal white bands; white streak starts above bill and goes to eye; clean white 'armpits' in flight
Similar Species:	Guillemot, Puffin, Little Auk
Size:	37–39 cm (14⅝–15⅜ in)
Habitat:	Inshore coasts, cliffs and islands; at sea in winter
Population:	Common

Puffin

This engaging and colourful sea bird is not easy to see. Although it breeds in large colonies in certain sites, it is only present for a few months of the year (March to July) and then quickly, almost instantaneously, disappears out to sea, often well out of sight of land – it has been known to cross the Atlantic. But wherever it occurs, it makes a very popular attraction. The upright posture and comical gait have a certain human resonance, and the huge, brilliantly patterned bill make it look like a dumpy, sea-living parrot.

The main breeding habitats for Puffins are tall cliffs and offshore islands, where they nest in a rock crevice or, more frequently, a burrow. The latter is usually dug out by the birds themselves, using their feet, and it is up to 2 m (6.5 ft) long. Not surprisingly, Puffins usually require the turf on top of cliffs rather than living on the cliffs themselves.

Fish Tricks

As in many auks, there is only one egg, laid in the burrow amidst a sparse lining of grass and root fragments, feathers and other dry material. Both sexes incubate for 39–43 days, with shifts of about 32 hours each, and the chick hatches with a covering of down.

Puffins are celebrated for their neat trick of bringing in a lot of fish at the same time, all held crossways in the bill. They do this firstly by having backward-pointing edges to the bill, that hold the fish by friction, and by hooking their tongue around them. It is by no means unusual to see a Puffin bringing in 10 fish so arranged, although a remarkable 62 has been reliably recorded. The youngster leaves the nest when about two months old and more or less fully grown. It does so under cover of darkness, alone and unknown to its parents.

Scientific Name:	Fratercula arctica
Identifying Features:	Broad, colourful bill; white cheek; red legs; triangular eye-patch
Similar Species:	None
Size:	26–29 cm (10¼–11½ in)
Habitat:	Sea cliffs and islands; oceans
Population:	Numerous but local summer visitor

Rock Pipit

The Rock Pipit is similar to the other British pipits in appearance and sound, but the bird itself is special. Very few other small passerines share its unusual maritime habitat, even for short periods. It is this bird alone that will be alongside auks and Kittiwakes at their breeding cliffs, and it is this one alone that is likely to be at the feet of waders such as Turnstones as they feed along the seaweed-covered rocks by the seashore. As such, and for its tendency to be seen inland only occasionally, it is very unusual.

It is not much to look at, though – a small, streaky bird with rather long legs and a habit of running or walking rather than hopping. It is best distinguished from the very similar Meadow Pipit by its dark legs, rather broad streaks down the breast and its overall dark plumage. The call is fuller than that of the Meadow Pipit, like that same species but with a cold, and the Rock Pipit uses it sparingly, in contrast to the Meadow Pipit's attacks of panic.

Flight

In some ways its lifestyle is similar to other pipits. For example, the male performs a song-flight along party lines, flying up slowly as it delivers its trilling song, then returning to earth like a paper aeroplane, wings still, tail spread and with a twisting flight-path. The Rock Pipit also feeds in the typical manner for the family, wandering over the ground in an apparently aimless manner, intermittently picking at things. However, as might be expected a few unusual items enter the menu, including molluscs, worms, crabs and small fish.

The Rock Pipit nest is placed inside a hole in a cliff or sometimes under dense vegetation and, besides the usual ingredients of grass and leaves, there is usually some seaweed in the structure. The female lays between four and six eggs.

Scientific Name:	Anthus petrosus
Identifying Features:	Streaky plumage; dark legs; buff outer tail feathers; dark bill
Similar Species:	Water Pipit, Meadow Pipit, Tree Pipit
Size:	16.5–17 cm (6½–6¾ in)
Habitat:	Rocky coasts
Population:	Common

Useful Addresses

British Trust for Ornithology
The Nunnery
Thetford
Norfolk
IP24 2PU
Tel: 01842 750050
www.bto.org

The Countryside Agency
Natural England
Northminster House
Peterborough
PE1 1UA
Tel: 0845 600 3078
www.naturalengland.org.uk

Forestry Commission
231 Corstorphine Road
Edinburgh
EH12 7AT
Tel: 0131 334 0303
www.forestry.gov.uk

The National Trust
PO Box 39
Warrington
WA5 7WD
Tel: 0870 458 4000
www.nationaltrust.org.uk/main/

**Royal Society for the
Protection of Birds (RSPB)**
The Lodge
Potton Road, Sandy
Bedfordshire SG19 2DL
Tel: 01767 680551
www.rspb.org.uk

Bird Observatories Council (BOC)
Department of BioSyB
National Museum Wales
Cardiff
CF10 3NP
Tel: 029 2057 3233
www.birdobscouncil.org.uk

British Ornithologists Union
PO Box 417
Peterborough
PE7 3FX
www.bou.org.uk

Scottish Ornithologists Club
Waterston House, Aberlady
East Lothian EH32 0PY
Tel: 01875 871330
www.the-soc.org.uk

Wildfowl and Wetlands Trust
Slimbridge
Gloucestershire GL2 7BT
Tel: 01453 891900
www.wwt.org.uk

Worldwide Fund for Nature
Panda House
Weyside Park, Godalming
Surrey GU7 1XR
Tel: 01483 426444
www.wwf.org.uk

Further Reading

Beddard, Roy, *The Garden Bird Year: A Seasonal Guide to Enjoying the Birds in Your Garden*, New Holland (London, UK), 2007

Beletsky, Les, *Collins Birds of the World: Every Bird Family Illustrated and Explained*, HarperCollins (London, UK), 2007

Birdlife International, *Bird: The Definitive Visual Guide*, Dorling Kindersley (London, UK), 2007

Brown, Roy; Ferguson, John; and Lees, David, *Tracks and Signs of the Birds of Britain and Europe*, Christopher Helm (A&C Black) (London, UK), 1999

Burton, Robert, *Garden Bird Behaviour*, New Holland (London, UK), 2005

Cocker, Mark and Mabey, Richard, *Birds Britannica*, Chatto and Windus (London, UK), 2005

Cook, Katrina and Elphick, Jonathan, *Birds*, Quercus (Colchester, UK), 2007

Couzens, Dominic and Partington, Peter, *Secret Lives of British Birds*, Christopher Helm (A&C Black) (London, UK), 2006

Couzens, Dominic, *Bird Migration*, New Holland (London, UK), 2005

Couzens, Dominic, *Identifying Birds by Behaviour*, HarperCollins (London, UK), 2005

Couzens, Dominic, *The Complete Back Garden Birdwatcher*, New Holland (London, UK), 2005

Couzens, Dominic, *The Secret Life of Garden Birds*, Christopher Helm (A&C Black) (London, UK), 2004

Flphick, Jonathan (Ed.), *Atlas of Bird Migration*, Natural History Museum (London, UK), 2007

Eppinger, Michael, *Field Guide to Birds of Britain and Europe*, New Holland (London, UK), 2006

Farrow, Dave, *A Field Guide to the Bird Songs and Calls of Britain and Northern Europe*, Carlton Books (London, UK), 2008

Greenoak, Francesca, *British Birds: Their Names, Folklore and Literature*, Christopher Helm (A&C Black) (London, UK), 1997

Harrap, Simon and Nurney, David, *RSBP Pocket Guide to British Birds*, A&C Black (London, UK), 2007

Holden, Peter and Cleeves, Tim, *RSPB Handbook of British Birds*, Christopher Helm (A&C Black), 2006

Hume, Rob and Hayman, Peter, *Bird: The Ultimate Illustrated Guide to the Birds of Britain and Europe*, Mitchell Beazley (London, UK), 2007

Hume, Rob, *RSPB Birds of Britain and Europe*, Dorling Kindersley (London, UK), 2006

Kettle, Ron and Ranft, Richard (Ed.s), *British Birdsounds*, British Library Publishing (London, UK), 2006

Lambert, Mike and Pearson, Alan, *British Birds Identification Guide*, Flame Tree Publishing (London, UK), 2007

Moss, Stephen, *Everything You Always Wanted to Know About Birds … But Were Afraid to Ask*, Christopher Helm (A&C Black), 2005

Moss, Stephen, *How to Birdwatch*, New Holland (London, UK), 2006

Moss, Stephen, *The Garden Bird Handbook: How to Attract, Identify and Watch the Birds in Your Garden*, New Holland (London, UK), 2006

Sample, Geoff, *Bird Songs and Calls of Britain and Northern Europe*, HarperCollins (London, UK), 1996

Sterry, Paul, *Complete British Birds: Photoguide*, HarperCollins (London, UK), 2004

Svensson, Lars and Grant, Peter J., *Collins Bird Guide: The Most Complete Guide to the Birds of Britain and Europe*, HarperCollins (London, UK), 2001

Ward, Mark, *Bird Identification and Fieldcraft*, New Holland (London, UK), 2005

Glossary

Altricial Unable to move around without assistance after hatching.

Archaeopteryx The earliest known fossil bird, the first example of which was discovered in 1861. This find proved that reptiles with feathers lived around 150 million years ago, forging a link between reptiles and birds.

Aves The bird class of vertebrates. Aves have feathers and most are able to fly. They are warm-blooded and lay eggs.

Avifauna The birds of a particular region or time.

Carrion Dead and decaying flesh. Birds of prey will feast on carrion, although they prefer to catch their prey live.

Cere A fleshy covering over part of the upper mandible.

Cline When a bird population shows a variation in certain characteristics such as weight or colour across its geographic range.

Cloaca The opening for digestive, reproductive and excretory systems in a bird.

Clutch The number of eggs a bird lays at any one time.

Coniferous woodland Woodland made up mainly of needle-leaved trees with cones. These trees retain their covering all year round.

Convergent evolution The process of evolution through which birds that are unrelated come to share similar characteristics and features.

Deciduous woodland Woodland made up of trees that lose their leaves in the autumn and throughout the winter.

Divergent evolution The process of evolution whereby birds that once shared similar characteristics have adapted over time and developed different ones in order to survive in changing habitats.

DNA Deoxyribonucleic acid. The material contained inside the nucleus of human and animal cells that contains all the genetic information.

Dromaeosaur Literally, 'running reptile', a group that includes dinosaurs such as velociraptors.

Ecosystem A self-contained habitat defined by the organisms living there and their relationships with one another and non-living factors such as climate and soil.

Endemic Found only in one place – birds that cannot be found in any other country. Most countries have a number of endemic species, but the Scottish Crossbill is the only bird endemic to the British Isles.

Extinction The process by which an animal or plant dies out completely. Some birds have been hunted to extinction by human predators; others have become extinct by natural selection or destruction of habitats. Conservation efforts are being made to prevent some endangered species from becoming extinct.

Fledge The growth of the first set of feathers of a baby bird. At this point the birds are known as fledglings.

Fossil The remains of an organism from a period in history, such as a skeleton or imprint of some flora, embedded in the crust of the earth.

Game bird Any bird that is hunted for sport. In Britain, grouse and pheasants are the most popular and widespread game birds.

Gape The expanse of a bird's open bill.

Hirundines Members of the swallow family.

Hybridization The cross-breeding of certain species with others to create a new species with certain characteristics.

Lekking An elaborate display ritual performed by male birds during the breeding season in order to attract a mate and drive off other potential suitors. Leks often take place in specific areas. The females watch the display before entering the lek to mate with the dominant male.

Mandible The jaws of a bird. Mandibles comprise two parts – upper and lower.

Mobbing A technique carried out by a group of birds, usually of the same species, to protect territory or young by driving out alien predators, by which the birds encircle and attack the alien.

Monophyletic species Pertaining to a group of animals or birds that are descended from one stock or source.

Nestling A young bird that has not yet fledged (grown its first set of feathers).

Nominate form The main form that a species takes. The same species may differentiate from the nominate form across a geographic region through divergent evolution.

Non-monophyletic species Pertaining to a group of animals or birds that are not descended from a single stock or source.

Palaeontologist A scientist who studies prehistoric forms of life through fossils and other evidence.

Pelagic Pertaining to birds that live on the open sea rather than in coastal areas or other regions of inland water.

Planform The shape of a wing (usually relating to its shape as seen from above).

Plumage The type and colouring of feathers on a bird; this can often change between seasons and differ between males and females of the same species.

Precocial Used to describe young birds that develop early and are able to perform functions such as moving about and even flying soon after hatching.

Predation The act of one bird preying and feeding upon another.

Primaries The large, main feathers situated on the distal joint of a bird's wing.

Quadruped Any creature that walks on four legs.

Race Also called subspecies. Made up of a population that has been dispersed geographically and has evolved its own distinguishable set of characteristics such as plumage or migratory habits; such populations can still breed with one another.

Raptor A bird of prey.

Remiges A type of feather that includes both primaries and secondaries; remiges are the feathers that are used in flight.

Resident A bird that lives and breeds in a country and does not make seasonal migrations.

Roding The process of cutting rushes or reeds to create a nest, used by water birds.

Scrape A shallow nest in the ground, usually simply scraped out of the mud or earth; used by ground-nesting birds such as plovers.

Secondaries The feathers that grow along the trailing edge of a bird's wings.

Substrate A surface on which an organism grows.

Taxonomy The science of classifying animals and birds according to a system that is defined by natural relationships and common characteristics.

Theropod Any of the carnivorous dinosaurs, literally meaning 'beast-footed'.

Tubenoses A group of sea birds with large tubular nostrils situated on the upper bill, allowing them to dive for fish.

Vagrant A migrant bird that has strayed from its typical migratory path and can therefore be seen in areas in which it is not normally resident.

Index of Latin Names

A

Accipter nissus 74–75
Acrocephalus
    schoenobaenus 194–95
Acrocephalus scirpaceus
    196–97
Actitis hypoleucos 184–85
Aegithalos caudatus 94–95
Aix galericulata 160–61
Alauda arvensis 126–27
Alca torda 240–41
Alcedo atthis 186–87
Alectoris rufa 110–11
Anas clypeata 166–67
Anas crecca 162–63
Anas platyrhynchos 164–65
Anthus petrosus 244–45
Anthus pratensis 130–31
Apus apus 38–39
Ardea cinerea 174–75
Arenaria interpres 216–17
Aythya fuligula 168–69

B

Branta canadensis 158–59
Buteo buteo 116–17

C

Calidris alpina 218–19
Carduelis cannabina 148–98
Carduelis carduelis 66–67
Carduelis chloris 64–65
Certhia familiaris 100–101
Charadrius hiaticula 214–15

Columba livia 32–33
Columba oenas 122–23
Columba palumbus 34–35
Corvus corone 146–47
Corvus frugilegus 144–45
Corvus monedula 104–5
Cygnus olor 156–57

D

Delichon urbica 40–41
Dendrocopus major 80–81

E

Emberiza citrinella 150–51
Emberiza schoeniclus
    198–99
Erithacus rubecula 46–47

F

Falco tinnunculus 118–19
Fratercula arctica 242–43
Fringilla coelebs 62–63
Fulica atra 176–77
Fulmarus glacialis 206–7

G

Gallinago gallinago 180–81
Gallinula chloropus 178–79
Garrulus glandarius 102–3

H

Haematopus ostralegus
    212–13
Hirundo rustica 128–29

L

Larus argentatus 228–29
Larus canus 224–25
Larus fuscus 226–27
Larus marinus 230–31
Larus ridibundus 222–23

M

Milvus milvus 114–15
Motacilla alba 192–93
Motacilla cinerea 190–91
Muscicapa striata 92–93

N

Numenius arquata 220–21

P

Parus ater 96–97
Parus caeruleus 54–55
Parus major 56–57
Passer domesticus 60–61
Phalacrocorax carbo 210–11
Phasianus colchicus 112–13
Phylloscopus collybita 86–87
Phylloscopus trochilus
    88–89
Pica pica 142–43
Picus viridis 78–79
Podiceps cristatus 172–73
Prunella modularis 44–45
Pyrrhula pyrrhula 68–69

R

Regulus regulus 90–91

Riparia riparia 188–89
Rissa tridactyla 232–33

S

Saxicola rubetra 132–33
Saxicola torquata 134–35
Sitta europaea 98–99
Sterna hirundo 234–35
Sterna paradisaea 236–37
Streptopelia decacto 36–37
Strix aluco 76–77
Sturnus vulgaris 58–59
Sula bassana 208–9
Sylvia atricapilla 82–83
Sylvia borin 84–85
Sylvia communis 140–41

T

Tachybaptus ruficollis 170–71
Tadorna tadorna 204–5
Tringa totanus 182–83
Troglodytes troglodytes
    42–43
Turdus iliacus 138–39
Turdus merula 48–49
Turdus philomelos 50–51
Turdus pilaris 136–37
Turdus viscivorus 52–53
Tyto alba 124–25

U

Uria aalge 238–39

V

Vanellus vanellus 120–21

Index

A

albinism 24

Arctic Tern 236–37

auks

Guillemot 238–39

Puffin 242–43

Razorbill 240–41

B

Barn Owl 124–25

birds of prey

Buzzard 116–17

Kestrel 118–19

Peregrine Falcon 30

Red Kite 114–15

Sparrowhawk 74–75

Black-headed Gull 222–23

Blackbird 48–49

Blackcap 82–83

Blue Tit 54–55

Bullfinch 68–69

buntings

Reed Bunting 198–99

Yellowhammer 150–51

Buzzard 116–17

C

Canada Goose 158–59

Carrion Crow 146–47

Chaffinch 62–63

Chiffchaff 86–87

Coal Tit 96–97

Collared Dove 36–37

colourings 24

Common Gull 224–25

Common Redshank 182–83

Common Sandpiper 184–85

Common Snipe 180–81

Common Tern 234–35

Common Whitethroat 140–41

Coot 176–77

Cormorant 210–11

Crossbill 72

crows

Carrion Crow 146–47

Jackdaw 104–5

Jay 102–3

Magpie 142–43

Rook 144–45

Cuckoo 130, 196

Curlew 220–21

D

doves

Collared Dove 36–37

Rock Dove 32

Stock Dove 122–23

ducks

Mallard 164–65

Mandarin Duck 160–61

Shelduck 204–5

Shoveler 166–67

Teal 162–63

Tufted Duck 168–69

Dunlin 218–19

Dunnock 44–45

E

escaped birds 24

F

Feral Pigeon 32–33

Fieldfare 136–37

finches

Bullfinch 68–69

Chaffinch 62–63

Goldfinch 66–67

Greenfinch 64–65

Linnet 148–98
Flycatcher, Spotted 92–93
Fulmar 206–7

G
gamebirds
    Partridge, Red-legged 110–11
    Pheasant 112–13
Gannet 208–9
Garden Warbler 84–85
Goldcrest 90–91
Goldfinch 66–67
Goose, Canada 158–59
Great Black-backed Gull 230–31
Great Crested Grebe 172–73
Great Spotted Woodpecker 80–81
Great Tit 56–57
grebes
    Great Crested Grebe 172–73
    Little Grebe 170–71
Green Woodpecker 78–79
Greenfinch 64–65
Grey Heron 174–75
Grey Wagtail 190–91
Guillemot 238–39
gulls
    Black-headed Gull 222–23
    Common Gull 224–25
    Great Black-backed Gull 230–31
    Herring Gull 228–29
    Kittiwake 232–33

Lesser Black-backed
    Gull 226–27

H
habitats
    coast 202
    freshwater and marshland 154
    open country 108
    urban and suburban areas 30
    woodland 72
Hedge Sparrow 44–45
Heron, Grey 174–75
Herring Gull 228–29
House Martin 40–41
House Sparrow 60–61

I
identifying birds
    behaviour 18
    features 14–18
    location 20
    sounds 20

J
Jackdaw 104–5
Jay 102–3
juvenile birds 22–24

K
Kestrel 118–19
Kingfisher 186–87

Kite, Red 114–15
Kittiwake 232–33

L
Lapwing 120–21
larks: Skylark 126–27
Lesser Black-backed Gull 226–27
Linnet 148–49
Little Grebe 170–71
Long-tailed Tit 94–95

M
Magpie 142–43
Mallard 164–65
Mandarin Duck 160–61
martins
    House Martin 40–41
    Sand Martin 188–89
Meadow Pipit 130–31
Mistle Thrush 52–53
Moorhen 178–79
Mute Swan 156–57

N
Nuthatch 98–99

O
owls
    Barn Owl 124–25
    Tawny Owl 76–77
Oystercatcher 212–13

P

Partridge, Red-legged 110–11
Peregrine Falcon 30
Pheasant 112–13
Pied Wagtail 192–93
pigeons
    Collared Dove 36–37
    Feral Pigeon 32–33
    Stock Dove 122–23
    Wood Pigeon 34–35
pipits
    Meadow Pipit 130–31
    Rock Pipit 244–45
Plover, Ringed 214–15
plumage, juvenile 22–24
Puffin 242–43

R

Razorbill 240–41
Red Kite 114–15
Red-legged Partridge 110–11
Redshank, Common 182–83
Redwing 138–39
Reed Bunting 198–99
Reed Warbler 196–97
Ringed Plover 214–15
Robin 46–47
Rock Dove 32
Rock Pipit 244–45
Rook 144–45

S

Sand Martin 188–89
Sandpiper, Common 184–85
Sedge Warbler 194–95
Shelduck 204–5
Shoveler 166–67
Skylark 126–27
Snipe, Common 180–81
Song Thrush 50–51
songs and calls 20
Sparrow, Hedge 44–45
Sparrow, House 60–61
Sparrowhawk 74–75
Spotted Flycatcher 92–93
Starling 58–59
Stock Dove 122–23
Stonechat 134–35
Swallow 128–29
Swan, Mute 156–57
Swift 38–39

T

Tawny Owl 76–77
Teal 162–63
terns
    Arctic Tern 236–37
    Common Tern 234–35
thrushes
    Mistle Thrush 52–53
    Song Thrush 50–51

tits
    Blue Tit 54–55
    Coal Tit 96–97
    Great Tit 56–57
    Long-tailed Tit 94–95
Treecreeper 100–101
Tufted Duck 168–69
Turnstone 216–17

W

wagtails
    Grey Wagtail 190–91
    Pied Wagtail 192–93
warblers
    Blackcap 82–83
    Chiffchaff 86–87
    Garden Warbler 84–85
    Goldcrest 90–91
    Reed Warbler 196–97
    Sedge Warbler 194–95
    Willow Warbler 88–89
Whinchat 132–33
Whitethroat, Common 140–41
Willow Warbler 88–89
Wood Pigeon 34–35
woodpeckers
    Great Spotted Woodpecker 80–81
    Green Woodpecker 78–79
Wren 42–43

Y

Yellowhammer 150–51